CONTACT JUGGLING

2nd Edition

JAMES ERNEST

Contact Juggling
2nd Edition

James Ernest

Typesetting and design by Nancy Hanger (Windhaven Press, Auburn, NH)
Published by Ernest Graphics Press
2530 East Miller Street, Seattle Washington 98112

Second Edition, 1991

ISBN   0-9634054-0-3

10 9 8 7 6 5 4

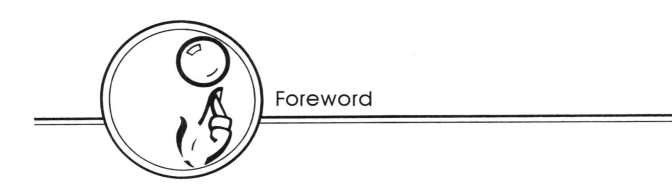

Foreword

This book is designed to provide instruction in the various tricks of contact juggling, an unusual juggling style which is both elegant and impressive. Many of the fundamentals of juggling theory are also covered, including methods for creating and learning new tricks in this and other styles.

I am indebted to the Society for Creative Anachronism for providing me with an audience whenever I've wanted to perform, and to Michael Moschen, whose contributions to the film *Labyrinth* first inspired me to learn contact juggling.

I am also grateful to my students for helping me expand the style and learn how to teach it. Most specifically I thank Richard Shumaker for his innumerable contributions to this book, including the Walking Cascade, Double-Butterfly Folding, and research into the methods and materials for Multi-Ball Palm Spinning.

Unlike most juggling textbooks, this one presupposes a little familiarity with the basics of the art. Except for the two basic lessons in Appendix II, I have done little to teach other forms of juggling, or even to describe them in detail. If you are unfamiliar with any of the concepts to which I refer, I would suggest checking out any of the juggling books in my suggested reading list.

Contents

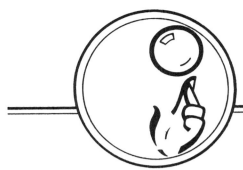

Introduction

What is Juggling?

There are many ways to define "juggling." If you ask most people what juggling is, they will tell you (more or less physically) that it is throwing and catching things. This is also the dictionary definition:

> Juggle: v. 1. To keep (two or more objects) in the air at one time by alternately throwing and catching them. 2. To manipulate in order to deceive. [Lat. *joculari*, to jest.] (*American Heritage Dictionary*, New York: Dell Pub. Co., 1983.)

As anyone who studies juggling will tell you, this describes only one of the many styles. In fact, the common man's definition secretly includes most of these other tricks: Devil Sticks, balancing, plate spinning, cigar box juggling, hat manipulation, etc. Even though he couldn't conjure up all these examples, he wouldn't be surprised to see a "juggler" doing them. The definition he is unconsciously using may be a little more like this:

> Juggle: To perform a visually complex and/or physically challenging feat using one or more inanimate objects as principals, which most people do not know how to do, and which furthermore has no real purpose other than entertainment, where the methods of manipulation are not mysterious (see Magic). Ex. Throwing and catching things.

Figure I.1
Balancing and Plate Spinning, from illustrations in the margins of Gothic manuscripts. Both are circa 1280 A.D.

While this is certainly a more detailed description, it still doesn't tell us much about juggling. It is a definition constructed mostly of negatives and general terms, rather like defining an elephant by saying it is a gray thing which is neither an apple nor a train. So, we are still asking, what is juggling?

Jugglers, who need to know, break their techniques into categories, usually grouping tricks by the kind of object used. I prefer to use a similar approach, but my divisions are based not on the props (for example clubs, hats, or hoops) but on the kind of manipulation being done. Here are some examples of various groups which, though neither comprehensive nor discrete, help paint a better picture of what jugglers do:

> "Toss" Juggling: Throwing and catching any number of things, usually in complex patterns. Ex. balls, clubs, axes, etc.

"Balancing": Maintenance of an object (or objects) in unstable equilibrium. This group also includes "setting," which is the maintenance of *stable* equilibrium. The difference here is between keeping a pool cue on your forehead, and doing the same with a salt shaker.

"Gyroscopic" Juggling: Taking advantage of the unusual properties of spinning objects. Ex. plates, balls, hula hoops, yo-yos, Diabolos, and some forms of Devil Stick and baton work.

"Contact" Juggling: Manipulations of single objects or object groups, usually involving very little tossing or spinning. Ex. balls, ball stacks, and some types of stick, hat, and plate work.

There are other styles, and other ways to regroup the various tricks listed above. For an expanded look at these and other categories, see Appendix 3, Understanding Juggling.

More about Contact Juggling

"Contact Juggling" is my own name for a style which fits only barely into the other categories of juggling, and which therefore deserves a name of its own. It is based, for the most part, on the manipulation of single objects.

The one-ball tricks in contact juggling involve rolling the ball from hand to hand, on the palm and the back, up the arms, across the chest, on the head, and elsewhere. The illusion created is one of a free-floating, weightless ball, subject to unusual laws of motion. A good contact juggler can make his own movements seem almost unrelated to the movements of the ball; the attention of the audience is always fixed on the ball. Contact juggling is, above all, graceful and absorbing.

The multiple-ball work described in this book is mostly in the same vein. Many of the moves involve treating several balls as a single object; others are based on simultaneously using a single ball (or ball group) in each hand. Therefore, contact juggling eight balls, a four-ball stack on each hand, is not as visually complex as toss juggling only three.

There are a few unusual moves which can be done with other items, which I have included in Chapter Eight. Although balls are the central focus of this book, a wealth of tricks are possible with hats, batons, hoops, knives, coins, and cards. I encourage you to experiment with them.

Contact juggling is not only one of the hardest forms of juggling to describe, but also one of the most tedious to learn. The basic move, the Butterfly, is one of the hardest, and unlike other styles, there is little you can show your friends after your first 20 hours of work.

If you do no other juggling, I would strongly suggest that you learn the basics of at least one other style while you work through this book. Try your hand at a three-ball cascade, walking Devil Sticks, or juggling with a hat and cane. This will relieve the monotony of your practice sessions, and will broaden the range of your hand-eye experience. Working on two or three styles at once can actually make each one a little easier to learn. It's the juggler's version of "cross-training."

It is the mesmerizing quality of contact juggling that truly separates it from other forms. To take a single ball and cause your audience to sit quietly amazed; to do something so simple and obvious and still hear, "How is that possible?"; this is the beauty of contact juggling. Juggling chain saws won't make them sit silently, and they won't ask you how you do it. Just why.

And, unlike producing a tiger from a fish tank, you can actually *tell* them how you do it, and they will still want to see it again.

A Note on the Technique of Learning Juggling: Take Small Steps

If you started with no juggling skill at all, and decided to learn how to balance a spinning plate on a pole, which is balanced on your forehead, while standing on one foot (Fig. I.2), you'd probably take it one step at a time. You would not, I think, take off one shoe, pitch a plate and a pole into the air, and hope. You'd break it into little steps.

But strangely, those same bright people who would never approach the pole-and-plate trick cold would try an even more difficult manipulation (the Butterfly, for example) without even a good idea of what the trick is supposed to look like. Stranger yet, people who deduce immediately that they should try juggling unlit fire torches before lighting them, will try to learn the basics of contact juggling with a $50 crystal ball.

Figure I.2
A Big Trick. This is actually a combination of three simpler tricks from Gyroscopics, Balancing, and Acrobatic Balancing

There is a reason for this. With some tricks, easier (and safer) versions of the final goal are not as obvious as they are in the examples above. Contact juggling in particular is very difficult to break into simple steps.

The Butterfly lesson is that not-so-obvious series of steps you need to take between incompetence and skill. You may even need to create smaller steps between mine, or you may want to add more to the beginning if, for example, you cannot hold a ball easily in your palm. If this sounds a little extreme, consider that one of my students is recovering from extensive hand surgery and is learning to juggle as a form of physical therapy.

The point is, don't get disappointed when your first attempts fail. Trying the Butterfly with no experience is really a lot like throwing a plate and a pole into the air and hoping. It is bound to produce a disappointing result. If your first attempt fails, and this goes for any juggling trick, try something similar but easier until you've truly mastered that. That's the way all juggling is learned: in small, simple steps.

And, I will add, that is why juggling books like this one are good things to have.

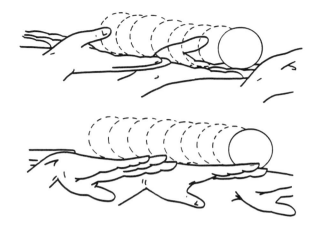

Part One
One Ball

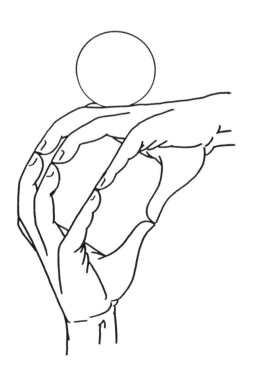

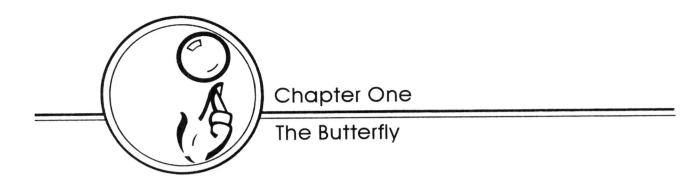

Chapter One

The Butterfly

The Butterfly is the essential move in Contact Juggling. A host of other moves are based on it, and it is the foundation of most one-ball routines. It is like the Cascade in Toss Juggling: it keeps the ball moving between tricks. But learning it can be a challenge.

When you learn to Toss Juggle, once you've "mastered" the three-ball Cascade (about a week of practice) you can go to the office and impress all of your friends. They will see you grin; they will think you have accomplished something wonderful. In fact, you have: you have impressed people with a trick that anyone can learn. Probably it is knowing this that makes you grin.

More importantly, in Toss Juggling, once you are over that first low hurdle, learning more tricks becomes intoxicatingly fun. The newer ones may be harder, but you already have an easy one to play with.

Learning to Contact Juggle can be a little more disappointing. It may take a month of hard work before you have even the most wobbly Butterfly in one hand. As with the Cascade, those first few hours are hard; but with the Butterfly, there are a lot more of them.

Stay with it.

The steps of the Butterfly are simple enough, and doing the first ones might even feel a little silly. But when you get to the next step and find it impossible, be prepared to do the silly stuff some more.

Also, although many of the advanced moves in this book are based on the Butterfly, there is no reason you shouldn't learn some other tricks while working on the Butterfly. Every trick you learn will teach you more about controlling the ball. Try to use the same "small steps" approach exemplified here when learning any complex trick.

The Butterfly, Step One: Hand Position

The Butterfly is named after a similar hand movement in Middle Eastern Dance (Fig. 1.1). Before you can keep a ball moving in the Butterfly pattern, you must learn where your hands go, so practice this first without a ball. Work on it slowly and carefully, with both arms at once. The move is like sending a wave up your arm, starting at the elbow.

Notice that this hand motion is not an exact copy of the actual Butterfly. Don't expect it to be. It basically serves to limber you up and get you used to moving your arms in these positions. Learn what every step looks and feels like. Remember, the beauty of Contact Juggling relies on the graceful movements of the body, as well as the ball.

Things to notice:

- Let the elbow lead the wrist, which in turn leads the fingertips. This means that when the elbow turns back out, the wrist is still moving in (Fig. 1.1f,g).

- Notice in the illustrations when the palm is up, and when it is down. Remember, the ball will ride on top of your hands throughout the Butterfly.

- Alternate your Lead Hand. In other words, one of your hands must cross closer to your body, while the other is out front. Alternate which is which. This will make the overall move more symmetrical, and will help you in the next chapter, Transfers. In the illustrations, the right hand is in the lead (Fig. 1.1a).

- Do this in front of a mirror, or with a friend. Find and correct your mistakes before they become bad habits.

- Keep your hands around chin level and your forearms in the same vertical plane. This "Wall Plane" can be represented by an imaginary wall about eight inches in front of you. Of course, you must break out of the wall plane a little to let your arms cross.

Step Two: Pitch and Catch

Now pick up your practice ball and ignore the pretty hand movements for a moment. The next step involves gaining a little control of the ball. (See Appendix I, Materials, for a discussion of good practice balls.)

Put your right hand in front of yourself, palm down, elbow out, as it would be in the Butterfly, Fig. 1.1a. This is the "Home" or "Central" Position for your hand: about six inches

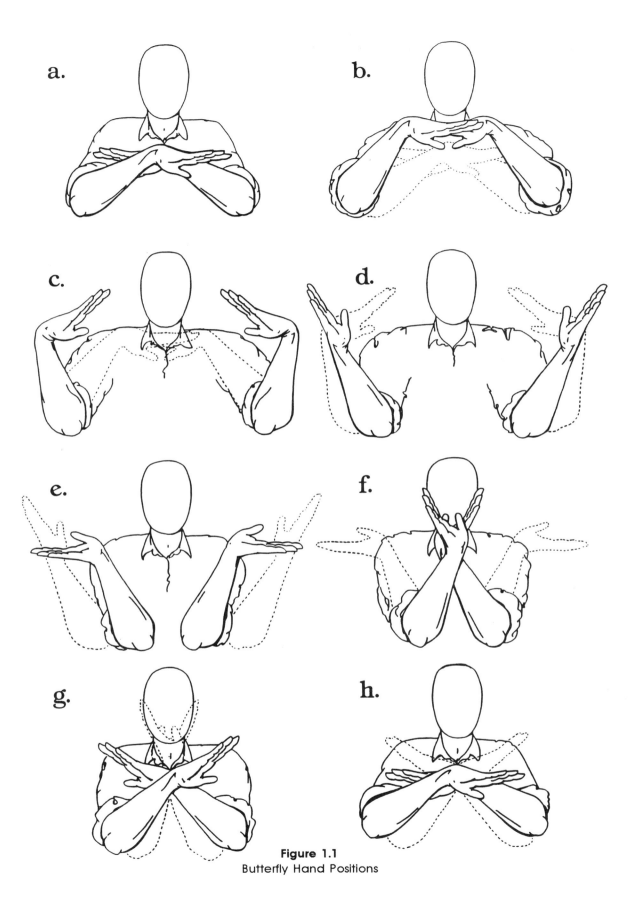

Figure 1.1
Butterfly Hand Positions

away from your chest, a little below shoulder level, with the elbow a little lower than the wrist (Fig. 1.3).

Hold the ball on the back of your hand. Don't grip it, but support it with three knuckles: the base of R3 and the first joints of R2 and R4 (see Fig. 1.2). Spread your fingers slightly, and lower R3 to let the ball rest comfortably. This position is called the "Cradle," and it is a standard hold used throughout Contact Juggling.

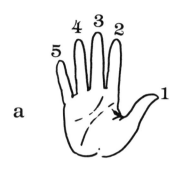

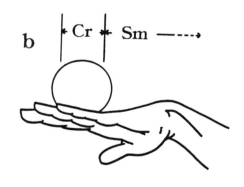

Figure 1.2
Parts of the hand: (a) Numbering the fingers, and (b) the "Cradle" and the "Smooth."

The Cradle is an area of relatively good control. Try to hold the ball anywhere past the base of the fingers (the "smooth" area of the hand) and you will have considerably less control. But with practice you can hold it comfortably in the Cradle.

To improve your control and confidence on the back of your hand, pitch the ball straight up about a foot, and catch it again in the Cradle, as in Fig. 1.3. This may be harder than it sounds, depending on how much of this you have tried before, but it won't take long to develop. Do whatever it takes to improve the dexterity on the back of you hand: try jiggling your arm a little and holding the ball, or try rolling it down onto the smooth part of your hand and back into the Cradle.

Remember to keep your hands near the Home position. You are not just training the back of your hand; you are training it *in* the Home position. I'm not telling you to strictly avoid other positions. I'm just reminding you to practice all the elements of this step.

Another thing to be working on at this stage is pitching and catching on the palm. Not directly out in front of you, where I assume you already can, but out to the side, where your hand would be palm-up in the Butterfly (Fig. 1.4).

Learn to pitch straight up and catch without moving your hand much, and without closing your fingers on the ball. Contact Juggling works best when the ball stays visible. This means not closing your hand or blocking the view in any other way. Of course, deciding when to break the rules will help make your routine unique.

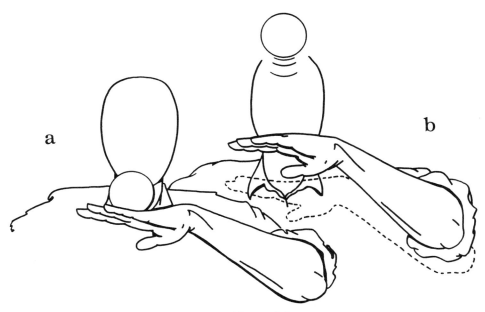

Figure 1.3
Pitch and Catch, inside.

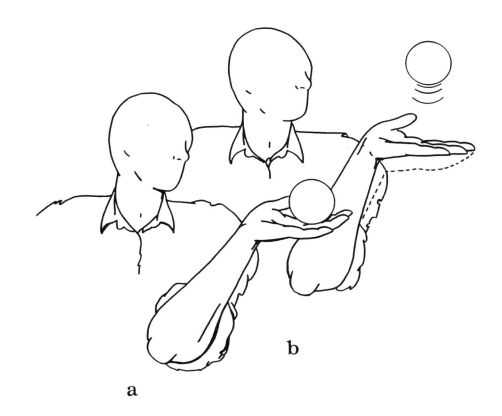

Figure 1.4
Pitch and Catch, outside.

Once you can pitch and catch in front of yourself on the back of your hand, and off to the side on your palm, you are ready to combine the two.

Put the ball on the back of your hand, in the Cradle. Toss it up, but not straight up. Throw it to the outside, and catch it on your palm (Fig. 1.5). Catch it as cleanly as you can in the outside position. Now, throw it back to the center and catch it in the Cradle. We're getting close, but don't get ahead of me.

Make this throw fairly high, about a foot. Don't worry about making it smooth yet, but be sure that you are catching the ball in the right places, not just catching wildly and then returning your hand to where it should be. Make sure your throws, in other words, are going to the right place.

Get this under control in both hands before you move on.

Figure 1.5
The Throw

Step Four: The Rolling Throw

When you can throw the ball from palm to back and from back to palm consistently, move on to the Rolling Throw (Fig. 1.6). This is a small but very important change from the simple throw. Instead of just throwing, make the ball roll from its resting position out to your fingertips before it leaves your hand. You're still putting the ball several inches into the air, but it's in contact with your hand for a longer time. The point of this exercise is to teach control of the roll on one side of the hand at a time. You should be able to get the ball rolling, from a dead stop, in the direction you want, before it leaves your hand.

After you feel comfortable with the Rolling Throw, with several inches of clearance between the ball and your hand, you can begin to lower the clearance. What you are ultimately trying to do is throw the ball so low (less than a quarter-inch from your fingertips) that it will roll down the other side into a catch. Even if this isn't very smooth yet, remember that you already have a lot more control than you used to. Just roll, catch, and stop. Start on the back of your hand, roll, catch on your palm, and stop. Take a breath. Now, roll from the palm to the back. Stop again. Once you have the two directions under control, you can put them together into the Butterfly.

Are you still working that bad hand as much as the good one? I knew you were. I was just making extra sure.

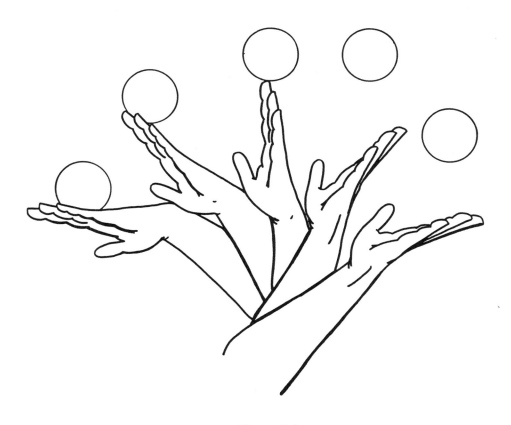

Figure 1.6
The Rolling Throw

Illustration 1.7 represents a full cycle of the Butterfly, from back to palm and back again. Be aware of the following things when practicing:

- The most common problem to have right now is the "High-Low" problem. It has some merit as a separate pattern, but right now you don't want to get stuck in it. The High-Low problem is this: When you have the ball in the outside position (on your palm) you're holding it about six or more inches higher than you will on the back of your hand (inside). The Butterfly, when done properly, moves the ball in a level figure-eight (on its side), or a level-footed arch, depending on your technique. The symmetry of this pattern is easy to destroy if you get lazy. Go back to the Butterfly hand position, watch yourself in the mirror, and get the move level again.

- Make sure that the hand stays fairly straight throughout the move. The wrist bends, not the fingers.

- The ball should be rolling right over your middle finger, at the tip. I once met someone who rolled the ball over the edge of his hand instead. He was twisting his wrist, not bending it. Put the ball up over the tips of your fingers.

- Don't let your fingers block the audience's view of the ball. If your audience is going to watch the ball, they have to be able to see it. Don't grip the ball in the Butterfly; support it.

- As in the hand movements, your elbow should be leading your wrist. Try doing this move with both hands at once. Keep the ball on one hand, and mirror the movements with your empty hand. When using both arms at once, make sure the forearms are operating in the same vertical plane, allowing space for them to cross. If you stray from the wall plane, transferring from one hand to the other will be tricky.

- Above all, smooth the move out. Make it fluid. Audiences fixate on the ball as long as it moves more like a bubble than a brick.

Figure 1.7
The Butterfly. (I've moved each image downward to make this illustration more clear.)

No two jugglers agree on how much practice time is reasonable, because different people work best under different conditions. Jugglers who are getting ready for international competitions are likely to want and need more daily practice than, say, you. Most people just can't imagine practicing for twelve hours a day.

Basically, if you are interested enough in what you are learning, you will make time, and it will pass quickly. When I was getting started, hours vanished before I could count them, because I was excited about learning. If you have to force yourself to practice, perhaps you should reconsider your choice of hobby.

On the other hand, if you become frustrated or do not advance after many hours of practicing, you may well be working too hard. Slow down, go steadily and comfortably, and above all, have fun. Sometimes your brain will process as much new information *between* practice sessions as it does during them. People who practice too much aren't letting their subconscious catch up!

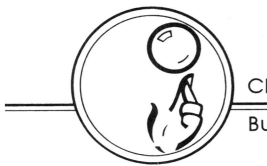

Chapter Two

Butterfly Transfers

1. The Palm-to-Palm

There are many different ways to roll the ball from one hand to the other, just as there are many toss juggling patterns possible with three balls. The easiest and most basic of these transfers is the Palm-to-Palm (P-P).

Hold the ball in the palm of your right hand. Roll it to the palm of your left hand. That's basically it. Now tell me you haven't done this before. Of course you have. And, by itself, this transfer is pretty dull.

To define it a little better, bring your palms up near the level where you do the Butterfly. Roll the ball back and forth, palm to palm, with the edges of your hands together as shown in Fig. 2.1. Get comfortable with it.

Now, to incorporate this transfer into the Butterfly, start with the ball on R. back, center of body (the home position for the Butterfly). Roll it over the fingertips to R. palm. Stop. At this point your palm should still be close to the center, not out to the side as in the basic Butterfly.

Do the new keen move. Stop.

Now, roll the ball from L. palm over the fingertips to L. back. This is actually a

Figure 2.1
The Palm-to-Palm transfer

little tricky, since you have to get the ball rolling from a dead stop. This problem goes away when you string all three moves together with no stops. Do that: back roll to palm, P-P transfer, palm roll to back. Stop. Lo, you have transferred the ball from hand to hand.

Now send it back.

This move is one of the exercises you should practice regularly, along with the Butterfly and the Back-to-Back transfer. Be sure to keep your bad hand in shape or else this move will become a little lopsided. Also, keep the mirror-image effect in mind: try moving your hands and arms in perfect sync as the ball moves from one to the other.

2. The Back-to-Back Transfer

The Back-to-Back transfer is more elegant than the Palm-to-Palm, and quite a bit more difficult.

Start the ball on the back of your left hand, in the Butterfly Home Position. Bring your right hand up in front of the left, in a position to catch (Fig. 2.2). For right now, put the right cradle directly in front of the left cradle. Let the ball roll straight away from you and into a catch.

We need to define a few terms at this point. The left hand in the exercise above is called the "throwing" hand, to keep it distinct from the right, or "catching" hand. The "cradle" is the area on the back of the hand where the ball is held, or kept in control. Call the area below the knuckles the "smooth" area, because a ball cannot be conveniently caught or held there. And remember: the hand further away from you is called the "lead" hand, meaning that if you walked forward, that hand would lead the other. In the Back-to-Back Transfer, the catching hand is always in the lead.

Figure2.2
The Back-to-Back transfer,
from the side.

Just roll the ball for a while, straight away from you, from cradle to cradle. Soon we will work with the smooth part, but stay in the cradles for the moment.

There are two reasons for rolling the ball forward (away from you) instead of towards your chest. First, the catching hand needs recovery space, and there is more room out in front. But more importantly, if you roll the ball towards your chest, the lead hand will block the audience's view. Once again, visibility is crucial. The roll-towards-self is a nice trick, and I won't tell you not to do it. Just don't do it right now.

Also, when you move your empty hand for the next transfer, bring it *under* the hand which holds the ball. Some people tend to move it over the ball instead, blocking the line of sight. You should discover that moving the empty hand under the other looks a lot smoother.

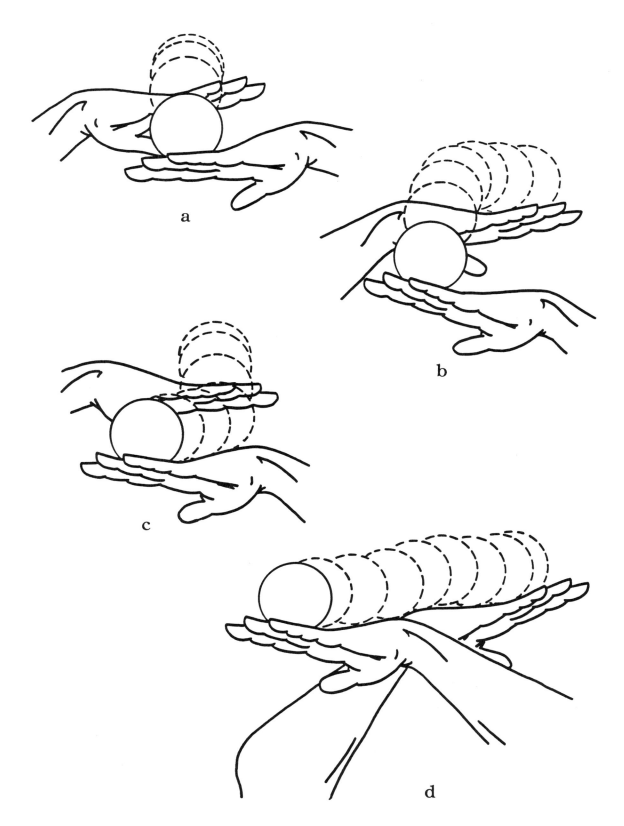

Figure 2.3
Four versions of the Back-to-Back: (a) straight away; (b) using the smooth of the throwing hand; (c) using the smooth of the catching hand; (d) using the smooths of both hands. Note: I've slightly lowered the catching hands in Figures a-c for clarity. The hands should be only slightly separated.

Now let's trek out onto the difficult, smooth part of the hand. On the smooth back of your hand you can't hold a ball very well, and it is even harder to stop or catch one here. If you are really ambitious, you might try learning to bring the ball down here during the Butterfly, but I have found that it isn't worth the extra effort.

If we can't catch or hold back here, what can we do? Roll through. Keeping a ball rolling through a low-control zone is easier than holding it still, just as it is easier to ride a bike down the street than it is to keep it still. Other areas of the body which will accommodate rolls include the entire arm, the chest, the shoulders, and even the legs and back. The head is a special case, because it is possible to catch and hold a ball on various places there. For more about these tricks, see Chapter Three, Isolations, Holds, and Rolls.

Stretch #1: Now we will begin to widen the pattern through which the ball rolls. Start with the ball held on the back of the right hand (in the cradle). Roll it down the hand towards the wrist, and then drop it straight into a catch in the left cradle (Fig. 2.3b). This is only a slight change from the first version of the Back-to-Back transfer: Now there is a little lateral movement.

Now send the ball back to the right cradle the same way. Roll from left cradle to left smooth, then drop into right cradle. Notice that the ball should go through the smooth without stopping; it only gets redirected in the control positions.

Stretch #2: Now start in the right cradle again. This time, set the ball down onto the smooth part of the left hand, and roll to a catch in the left cradle (Fig. 2.3c). This is similar to (b), but you are working with the smooth of the catching hand instead.

Stretch #3: This is the hardest variation. Roll the ball from the right cradle onto the right smooth, drop it off at about the wrist, onto the left smooth. Continue the roll into a catch in the left cradle (Fig. 2.3d). You have now stretched the cradles further apart, and made the Back-to-Back transfer a longer and more graceful roll; much more elegant than the cradle-to-cradle drop.

By the way, you've just learned your first non-Butterfly trick, the Staircase. For a more complete expansion of this trick, look it up in Chapter Three.

Now it is time to incorporate the Back-to-Back transfer. This is very much like what we did for the Palm-to-Palm. Start with the ball on your right palm, outside, as it would be in the Butterfly. Roll the ball over your fingertips to a catch on the right cradle, inside. Bring your left hand up in front of the right, for a Back-to-Back transfer. Stop.

Do the new keen move: the longest (most "stretched") Back-to-Back you feel comfortable with. It isn't necessary to do the entire cradle-smooth-smooth-cradle stretch, but it looks nicer if you can. Stop.

You are now ready to Butterfly with your left hand. Roll the ball over the fingertips to the left palm (outside). Stop.

You have now learned the important Back-to-Back transfer. Now do it again. Take out the stops, smooth it out, get it under control. This move and the Palm-to-Palm transfer are the

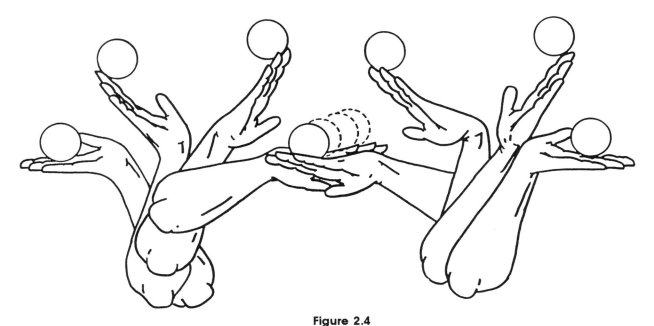

Figure 2.4

Incorporating the Back-to-Back transfer.

two most basic Butterfly transfers. They will strengthen your one-ball routine more than any other moves. Get them down cold, both ways, soon.

A Note on Combination Theory

Throwing a club under your leg and catching it, once, is one trick. Doing this while juggling three clubs is another trick. And, just as one quarter note sounds different from a series of them, a series of under-the-leg throws looks different from a single one. This, then, is another trick. We call this type a **series**: several repetitions of one move.

Two quarter notes of different tones, played either together or in sequence, sound different from a single one. Throwing a club behind the back right after throwing one under the leg is called a **combination**; a melody, if you will, of juggling tricks.

Figure 2.5
A simple musical series and combination.

Finally, continuously repeating a combination, such as leg-back-leg-back, is yet another trick. It is **a series of combinations**. Theoretically, there is an infinite number of combined series possible with only two tricks, just as a binary computer system can store most of the information in the world using only ones and zeros.

Of course, an audience can get tired of ones and zeros, be they in unique combinations or not.

The business of building a solid routine is like that of composing a symphony: how many times and in what combinations should I play the few notes (do the few tricks) available to me in order to create something pleasant, unique, and entertaining?

With this in mind, here are some possible combinations of the tricks we have learned so far:

1) Butterfly in one hand, constant. (Either hand.)

2) Repeated Palm-Palm transfers.

3) Repeated Back-Back transfers.

4) Circle (B-B followed by P-P, repeat.)

5) Longer combinations and series.

You might also do a Back-to-Back transfer, then a stall (a complete Butterfly), then another Back-to-Back. I usually improvise, both in practice and on stage, thinking about three moves ahead. When I am going for real unity, I will choreograph a series of twenty moves or so. When working with my own music, I write an entire routine.

In case it needs more explanation, the Circle (#4 above) is a series of alternating P-P and B-B transfers, which keep the ball rolling in what is basically a tight circle (see Fig. 2.6). If you do a Back-to-Back from left to right, and a Palm-to-Palm from right to left, the ball will go clockwise (from your perspective). Try both directions and get proficient with both of them. Since you never have to stop the ball completely, this is about the easiest Butterfly transfer move, and can therefore be done with wobbly shapes like fruit and vegetables, which we are for some reason often called upon to juggle.

Other Transfers

While we are still on the subject of Butterfly transfers, let us explore a few more of the possibilities. The first two are recombinations of the tricks we have already learned; the others will involve modifications of the basic Butterfly.

•Palm-to-Back Transfer:

Butterfly the ball from the back of your right hand to the palm, then let the ball continue rolling off the base of your palm onto the back of the left hand, into the cradle. From here, you might either reverse the ball's direction and send it back up over the left fingertips in another Butterfly, or let it

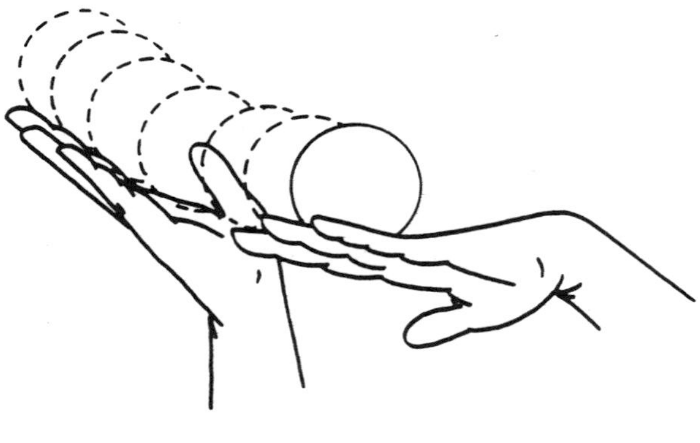

Figure 2.7
The Palm-to-Back transfer.

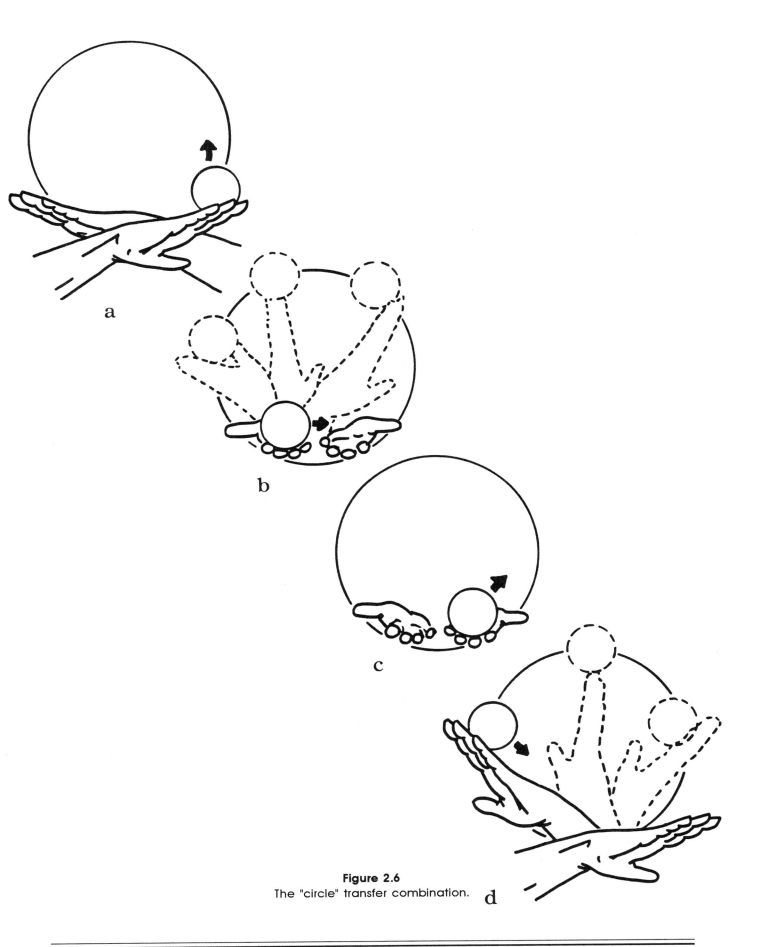

Figure 2.6
The "circle" transfer combination.

roll over the smooth of the left hand into a catch on the right cradle, in a Back-to-Back transfer.

A series of Palm-to-Back transfers is an interesting trick. Experiment by combining it with other similar tricks as well.

•Back-to-Palm Transfer:

This is basically a reversal of the Palm-to-Back configuration. You must give the ball a serious push to roll it up the back of the throwing hand and across the palm of the catching hand.

A series of these tends to climb, and looks really marvelous.

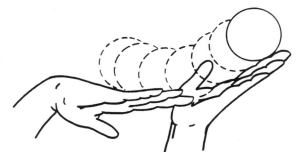
Figure 2.8
The Back-to-Palm transfer.

•Breaking the Wall Plane and other Butterfly Variations:

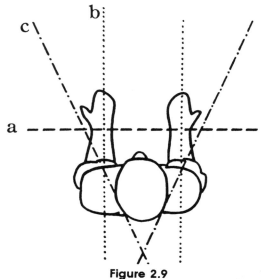
Figure 2.9
Various Butterfly Planes.

Although the "wall plane" is the easiest place for the Butterfly, you need not restrict yourself to it. For example, it is possible to move the ball within planes that extend directly in front of you, or in any planes that extend radially from your shoulders (Fig. 2.9 b,c).

You will notice when working in these planes that you have two options: you may want your palm up on the outside, down on the inside (at the shoulder), or vice versa. Either way, you will probably need to go through the same steps that you did for the basic Butterfly: hand movements alone, vertical tosses, throwing, and the rolling throw.

Figure 2.10
A Palm-down-outside Butterfly within plane (2.9b).

Although it may seem uncomfortable at first, you even have the palm up/palm down option in the wall plane. Unless you are very limber, however, the recovery space in the outside position (back of hand) is about zero.

•Twisting:

Since you have the option, in most cases, of having your palm up, try the following:

In the wall plane, start with your palm up, outside position (Fig. 2.11). Begin to Butterfly to the inside, but when the hand reaches vertical, twist your wrist and bring your hand down palm-up on the inside. With a little practice you can make this look very similar to the basic Butterfly.

Figure 2.11
The Twisting Butterfly.

When you try this with a ball, make sure the ball is getting up over your fingertips. Don't get lazy or it will look like you are just holding the ball and twisting your wrist.

Now that you have the ball palm-up on the inside, you may want to Butterfly-Twist back to where you started, or do the next transfer, the Inside Palm-to-Palm.

•The Inside Palm-to-Palm Transfer:

This transfer, also called "Crossed Arms" and the "Baby" transfer, is about the best reason to learn the Butterfly-Twist.

Hold your arms crossed, palms up, as if you were holding a baby (Fig. 2.12). Roll the ball from the top hand down the arm and drop in a catch on the other palm. Now move the empty hand under the other, and repeat the roll the other way. You can make a lovely staircase out of these transfers, especially if the ball rolls all the way to your fingertips before coming back.

Figure 2.12
The inside Palm-to-Pam transfer.

To incorporate this transfer into a Butterfly routine, begin with the ball on your right palm, outside. Butterfly-Twist to the inside (still on palm), do the transfer, and then do a reversed Butterfly-Twist in the left hand, from palm inside to palm outside. This is a very tricky combination.

•Easier versions of the Baby:

To make it a little easier, try this: a crossed-arm Palm-to-Back. Simply roll to the back of the catching hand, and Butterfly out (Fig. 2.13a).

Figure 2.13b
The inside Back-to-Palm.

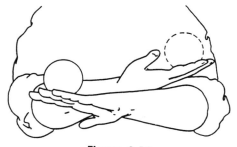

Figure 2.13a
The inside Palm-to-Back.

Or, try transferring from the back of the throwing hand to the palm of the catching hand (Fig. 2.13b).

Working on either of these simpler versions can help you with the inside Palm-to-Palm.

Build your own Variations:

If you combine the elements of breaking the plane, twisting your wrist, and crossing your arms, you should be able to concoct any number of new Butterfly transfers. Transfer from one plane to another, across the fingertips or the sides of your hands.

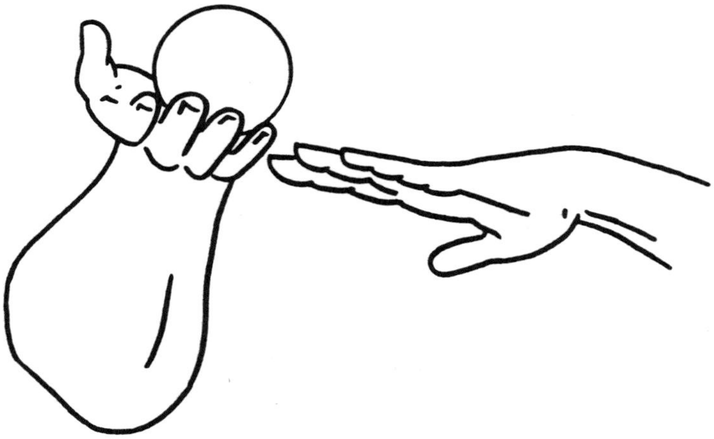

Don't be discouraged if the moves you invent seem (at first) impossible. If you can hold your hands in the necessary positions, you can learn the trick. Try to devise the simplest steps possible, like the ones you used in learning the basic Butterfly.

Figure 2.14
A transfer between two planes.

And remember: Butterflies and Butterfly transfers are only one of the many directions in which to expand.

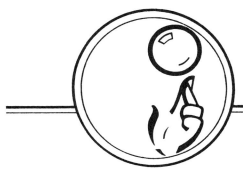

Chapter Three

Isolations, Holds, and Rolls

Isolations are moves which keep the ball essentially motionless while the hands are in motion. Holds are where both ball and hand are held still. Rolls are what we have mostly been discussing so far: the ball is moving, and usually the hand (or other support) is, too.

Isolations

•Palm Circle

The most elegant isolation, and one worth learning, is the (one-ball) Palm Circle.

Take a ball, the heavier the better, and put it on your palm. Spread your fingers a comfortable distance, and begin to move your palm in small circles. Find out which direction, clockwise or counterclockwise, feels more comfortable. Try to keep the ball still while your hand makes larger and larger circles (Fig. 3.1).

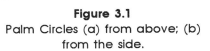

Figure 3.1
Palm Circles (a) from above; (b) from the side.

The isolation effect of one-ball Palm Circles relies on the inertia of the ball. If you were holding a greased pizza pan, and the ball were a smooth box, you could move the pan in circles without moving the box. That in itself is a neat thing to look at. Unfortunately, your hand is not a greased pizza pan, and the ball is not a box. Your hand is bumpy, and the ball is rolling instead of sliding, which gives you a different kind of friction to deal with.

This trick is one of the easiest to grasp, and one of the hardest to master. When I started, I discovered to my dismay that my left hand wasn't even capable of making horizontal circles. I had been juggling for many years, but when I tried to get an "O" out of my left hand, all I got were "L"s and "Z"s.

The benefits of learning this isolation actually outweigh the agony. The illusion works best if you do a few circles on each hand, and then start to change hands each round. Bring the catching hand up from below, and have it moving in circles even when the ball isn't on it. With both hands moving like this, a good contact juggler can make the ball seem to float. Just when your brain decides that it is sitting on the left hand, that hand drops away without the ball.

I have never seen circles done on the back of the hand. I imagine that, like most moves, when taken to the back of the hand it becomes even more impressive. And more difficult.

•Walking

Easier than Palm Circles is the set of isolations called "walks." In these, the ball is always rolling in one direction (relative to the hands), and is therefore always changing hands. It is the right-left-right-left feel of these isolations that gives them their name.

•1) Walk Away:

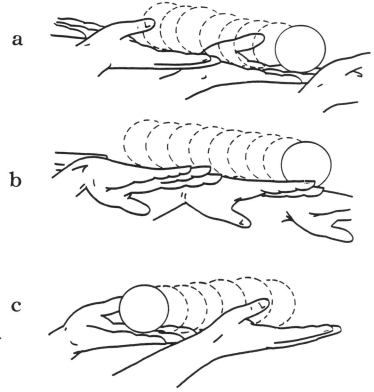

Hold your hands in front of you, as in Fig. 3.2 a, with the fingertips of the right hand touching the wrist of the left (catching) hand. Roll the ball away, onto the palm of the left hand, and reverse the hand positions. Repeat this walk as smoothly as possible, keeping the ball as steady as you can.

Now, turn one of your hands over and use the back. Go left-right, front-back for a while, training one hand at a time. Try to use as much of the smooth back of your hand as possible. When you get better on the back of each hand, try walking away only on the backs (Fig. 3.2b).

•2) Walk Towards:

This is just the reverse of the Walk Away (Fig. 3.2c). You will notice that, from the palms, it is quite easy to roll the ball up your arm before dropping it into a catch.

Figure 3.2
Three types of walks: (a) away on the palm, (b) away on the backs, (c) towards self on the palms.

Once again, practice palms-up first, then work the back of one hand at a time to gain control.

You can combine walking away and towards for some lovely effects. Try chasing the ball across the stage, making it glide away gracefully like a bubble.

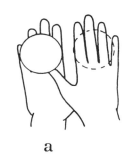

a

b

•3) Other Walks:

Besides walking away and towards, you can do walks from side to side. Do a regular Palm-to-Palm transfer, then cross your arms and transfer again in the same direction. Try the same on the backs of your hands. You should notice that, when your palms are down, your thumbs don't get in the way as much.

A nice odd walking effect is shown in Fig. 3.3. Do a Back-to-Back walk from right to left, cross arms, and transfer back to the right hand. Then, bring the right hand *around* the left in a small circle and repeat the move. Variations of this are possible in any walk; you are basically relocating the ball-in-hand instead of the empty hand. These moves cease being strictly isolations, but they fit closely with the other walking moves. By adding more circles and transferring in different directions, you can create a very complex walking routine.

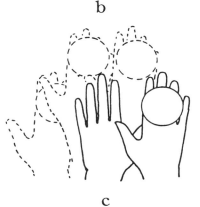

c

Figure 3.3
Another walking variation:
moving the Ball-in-Hand

Another variation of the walk is what I call Sidestepping. We will encounter this move again in multi-ball work.

Sidestepping is basically the same as the original walk away, except the hands no longer conform to a straight line.

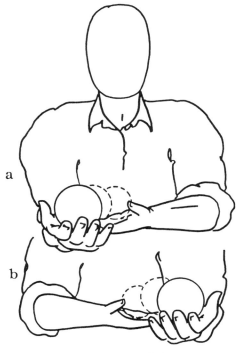

a

b

Figure 3.4
Sidestepping

When you hand the ball from right to left, do it on the left side of the straight away line. Then cross that line, and do the next transfer on the right side of it (Fig. 3.4). The ball is now swaying back and forth as you roll it away; a pretty little change from the basic walk.

Try side-to-side or even up-and-down versions of the walks you have already learned. Figure out what lines you are working in, and then break them! In a general sense, this is how new tricks are born.

Holds

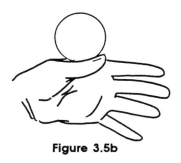

Basically, anywhere you can put the ball and keep it still is a good place for a hold. If you have a way to get it there and back, even better. Here are just a few possible holds (Fig. 3.5).

Figure 3.5a

a) Fingertips: This one is harder to get into than out of, so I usually begin my routine in this hold. An important consideration is tension: is your hand tense or relaxed? Is it a lot of work to keep the ball where it is, or is it a bubble in the air which you just happen to be touching? My style usually assumes the latter.

Figure 3.5b

b) Open Hand: Here is another hold where a relaxed appearance is essential. If you close your hand in this hold, you can roll directly into the Fist Hold (Fig. 3.5d).

c) Elbow: If you can roll the ball up and down your forearm fairly easily, and you have a good flat spot at your elbow (most people do), then you can bring the ball to rest at the crook of your elbow. Don't grip it; support it. From there you might roll it away, or pitch it into the air and catch it somewhere else: your palm, the cradle, on your fist, or even in the same hold again. One of my students likes to gently blow on the ball to "coax" it back down his arm.

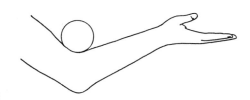

Figure 3.5c

d) Fist: An exception to my "relaxed" rule is the Fist Hold, since there is no such thing as a relaxed fist. It is the moving in and out of tension that makes this trick interesting. Try getting into this hold from the cradle by slowly closing your hand. Push this hold up to the top of your reach, or move it in slow circles.

Figure 3.5d

e) Head: It is difficult to roll a ball into this hold, so try placing it there or throwing it from your palm. Michael Moschen, one of the world's best contact jugglers, finishes his act by pitching a crystal ball onto his forehead, and while holding it there, lies down and goes to sleep. Don't try this with crystal unless you like being bruised!

A Note on Serendipity

Figure 3.5e

Every time you make a weird mistake, remember it. As with any random process, most of the mistakes you make will be foolish and useless. But every now and then you will come across something wonderful.

Once, when I was practicing the Chest Roll, I managed to accidentally catch the ball on my collarbone. I turned to the person with me and said, "Look, a beautiful new hold!" And it was. And the way I figured, if I could do it once, I could do it again. And I did.

Unfortunately, I couldn't figure how to get *out* of it without grabbing the ball, which, in contact juggling, is a pretty big no-no.

Pay attention to whatever weird mistakes you make. Turn them into tricks and show people. That's how some of the most unusual new moves are developed.

Rolls

Between any two control positions is a smooth place. Rolling through those smooth places is the heart and soul of a one-ball routine. You may do a lot of nice transfers and holds, but what the audience will probably remember most is how well (and where) you could roll the ball.

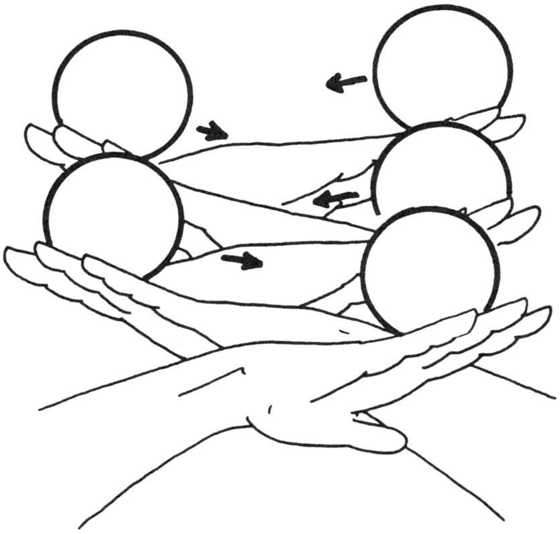

•The Staircase and the Escalator

The Descending Staircase is simply a series of Back-to-Back transfers, the smoother the better, with each slightly lower than the one before. Beginning well above eye level, the ball swoops slowly down to about waist level, taking wide and graceful steps. To do an Ascending Staircase, simply lift the catching hand a little higher after each transfer.

Figure 3.6a
The Descending Staircase

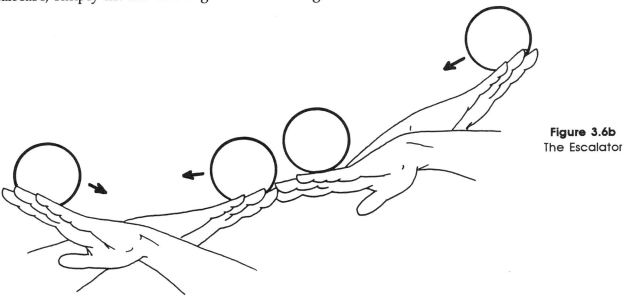

Figure 3.6b
The Escalator

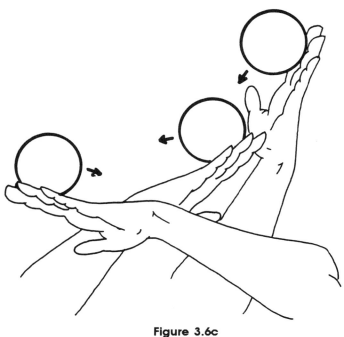

Figure 3.6c
Entering the Staircase from a Palm-to-Back transfer (chapter 2).

The wider you stretch your transfers, the better this trick will come off. Remember also the Baby Staircase: arms crossed, palms up, as in Fig. 2.12. Alternate these two, or combine them all into a Butterfly routine.

The Escalator is a stretched version of the Descending Staircase: instead of reversing the direction of the ball each time it reaches the cradle, do another transfer from tip-to-tip, back-to-back. Then at the next chance, turn the ball around (Fig. 3.6b). The path of the ball is a little broader in shape than the simple staircase, especially if you do a good job of isolating the hands during that long middle roll.

Of course, you can create your own pattern of switchbacks, or even go as far as to never turn the ball around, but instead turn yourself as you let it descend (or ascend) in a slow spiral around you. You may prefer, for this trick, to make the transfers side-to-side, rather than tip-to-tip and tail-to-tail. (This was one of the Walks.)

While we are on the subject of hand configurations, let's consider more ways to roll the ball from hand to hand. A lot of these are difficult to tell apart from the audience, but any one of them might lead to a new set of tricks.

Where can the ball leave the hand? Even if we treat only the four basic directions, we have eight places (four front and back) to leave, and eight places to enter. The ball can also enter and leave the same hand, as in the case of the basic Butterfly. If statistics inspire you, with the eight points of entry and exit, we have a matrix of 64 hand-to-hand combinations, six hand-to-same hand moves, and 4900 combinations of two such moves.

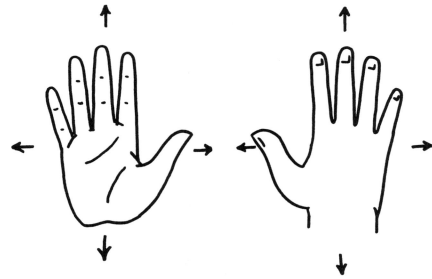

Figure 3.7
The right hand: directions the ball might go.

Once again, most of these look pretty much the same. But experiment with them. They just might lead you in completely new directions.

•Body Rolls

Along with rolls on your hand, there are many ways to roll the ball on your body. These tricks are, simply enough, called body rolls.

Arm: We have already discussed the Arm Roll: you needed it to get into the Elbow Hold (Fig. 3.5c). Remember, for all body rolls, it is easier to balance the ball while it is moving than to keep it supported in a hold. Just like riding a bicycle. Try rolling up and back without stopping at the elbow.

Back of the Arm: Starting with the ball in the cradle, you can send it all the way to your elbow and beyond before it falls off. Try this in the wall plane or straight out in front. In the wall plane, it is rather like stretching the Back-to-Back transfer beyond the wrist. Once the ball has reached your elbow, you can with some effort reverse its direction and send it back to the hand, palm or back. You might also pitch it into the air or roll it straight off to the other hand.

Chest: Although it is a juggler's juggling trick, one that is much harder than it looks, the Chest Roll (Fig. 3.8a) is one you may wish to learn. The ball begins, ideally, in the cradle of the right hand, rolls down the right arm, across the chest just below the chin (you must lean back a little to give the ball a level place to roll), and down the left arm to the left cradle. To learn this trick, you may want to borrow some sporting goods.

Figure 3.8a
Chest Roll.

Just as balancing a pool cue is easier than balancing a pen, body rolls are easier with a basketball than with 2" lacrosse balls. Learn the Chest Roll, as well as any other body rolls you can devise, with a basketball first. Experiment with what can be done; find out where you can control it.

Then, move down the size scale a bit. Use a volleyball, a softball, a lacrosse ball. This is just another method of taking small steps, like riding lower and lower bicycles or balancing shorter and shorter poles.

Back Roll: Start with a ball (a big one!) on the back of your right hand. Lean forward and roll the ball down your arm and across your back, to the other hand (Fig. 3.8b). You might also try catching it halfway, in the little well created by your shoulders and neck. From the neck catch you can throw it into the air or roll it over to your forehead. Bobby May

Figure 3.8b
Back Roll.

used to finish his routine by rolling the ball down his back (from the neck catch), and catching it between his legs while executing a forward somersault.

Leg-Back Roll: Once again, with a big ball start as shown in Fig. 3.8c, with the ball on your foot. Roll it up your leg to your hip. When the ball reaches your hip, twist away from it and roll it up your back, down one of your arms, and into a hold.

I know what you're thinking: "Then take off and fly down the road." But if you work as hard on this sort of trick as you did on the Butterfly, you really will see results! This illustration is taken from a photograph of Francis Brunn, who performed the roll I have described with a ball in each hand.

Figure 3.8c
Leg-Back Roll

Head Rolls: It is interesting that the Head Roll is performed by ten times as many jugglers as the Butterfly, even though it is just as hard, and makes you a lot dizzier. Henry VIII is said to have performed it, Bobby May popularized it early in this century, and jugglers worldwide have been expanding on it ever since.

In fact, the basic Head Roll is little more than an on-the-head Butterfly. The control positions are the temples, with another in the middle of your forehead, and the fourth on the back of your neck.

Just as you did when learning the Butterfly, move your head through all these positions before trying it with a ball! If you aren't limber enough to thrash around without the ball, you can really pull a muscle trying to learn the Head Roll.

Since you can hold a ball on your forehead, start there. Roll to a temple, then back to a hold on your forehead. This way, you work one side at a time. Try going from forehead to neck and back again. Now try a full Butterfly: temple-to-temple without a stop.

Figure 3.9
Head Rolls

This is one of those tricks with more variations than I can describe. Experiment with the possibilities.

Chapter Four

Other Tricks

Here are a few one-ball tricks which belong in classes by themselves.

The Mineshaft: Begin with the ball as shown in Fig. 4.1a, supported lightly by the fingertips of each hand. Let it slide slowly down into a hold between the palms, making sure that your pinkies don't close in and cover the ball. Now slowly drop your hands through part (b) into part (c), with the Mineshaft now facing down. Slide the ball down to your fingertips.

This is best when executed slowly, perhaps as part of a production. There is a point at the bottom of the Mineshaft where the ball looks like it will fall. You are basically supporting it with horizontal pressure from your middle fingers. The lower you can go, the better.

Billiard Ball Rolls: Along with the Mineshaft, there are many other ways to orient and move your hands with the ball gripped between them (Figs. 4.2a-c). Many of this type of hold are detailed in books of billiard ball magic. Several of them involve productions and vanishes, which are easier with smaller balls. A long combination of these moves is a nice way to begin your routine.

a

b

c

Figure 4.1
The Mineshaft

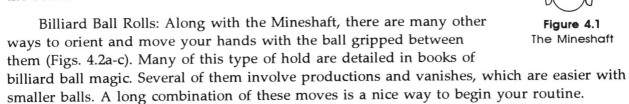

a

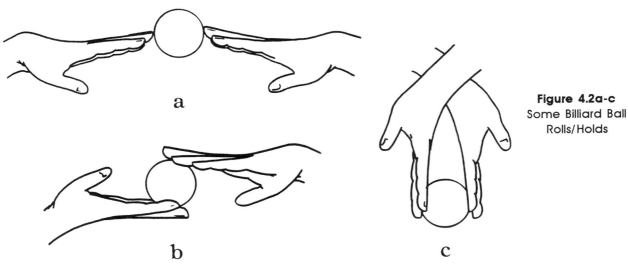

b

c

Figure 4.2a-c
Some Billiard Ball
Rolls/Holds

Back-and-Forth (the Wave): Put both hands together, palms up, fingers pointing away from you (Fig. 4.3, as seen from the front). Support the ball at your fingertips and roll it back and forth, raising the fingers slightly as it passes. Don't close the fingers, just raise them slightly. This gives the effect of waves on water, with a bubble floating on top. Check this move in a mirror; it looks much better to the audience than it looks to you.

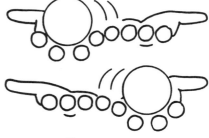

Figure 4.3
The Wave

The Elevator: This is getting pretty close to toss juggling. Hold your left hand, palm down, a few inches (or further) above your right hand, which holds the ball. Pitch the ball straight up, just hard enough so that it tops out at your left hand. Catch it. This is a very smooth move, if done properly, and gets a good response from the audience. It gives the ball a weightless look.

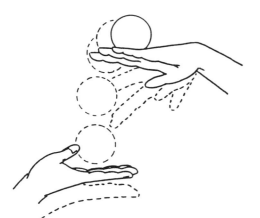

Figure 4.4
The Elevator

To get an idea of what this should look like, imagine dropping the ball from your left hand (doing the trick in reverse). Roll it from the cradle down the fingers, to fall through the air to a catch in the right hand. Now, run that image backwards. This trick is appealing because, done properly, it looks very much like a film running backwards.

You can catch the ball in the cradle, as shown here, or in a fist hold. You might also try catching the ball against your palm, gripping it with your thumb. It is the same type of reverse motion catch (if the ball comes to a stop before you grab it), but each has a slightly different look.

Thumb Hold: And while we're holding the ball with our thumb, try this little gag. Yes, contact juggling, for all of its elegance, lends itself to sight gags.

Figure 4.5
The Thumb Hold

Butterfly the ball in your right hand. Once, after a few repetitions, grab it with your thumb while it is on your palm, hold it there, and do another half-step in the Butterfly. It looks like the ball is sticking to your hand (Fig. 4.5), which will confirm the suspicions of several audience members who think you're using velcro. Even if you are using a crystal ball, there are a lot of places where your thumb cannot be seen. Make like the ball is really stuck, or wave it back and forth a little before you set it free.

Or, be serious and forget the gag. Stylistic choice.

Actually, being able to catch the ball this way will help you when you are inventing and learning multiple-ball transfers, which are discussed in Chapter Five.

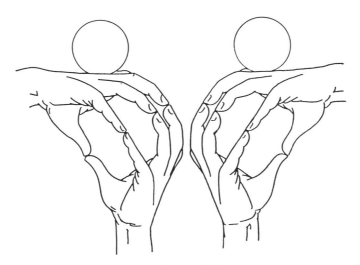

Figure 4.6
The Cage

The Cage: Make a cage by touching every fingertip of one hand to its match on the other (Fig. 4.6). Rest the ball on top of this cage, in the two-finger cradle between R.2 and R.3. Now, either:

- Move your hands around so that the ball ends up on your left palm, inside the cage, and the toss/roll it back out into the original hold, or

- Roll from the right cradle to the left cradle (along the fingers) without opening the cage. The difficult thing about this roll is that if you get the ball rolling very fast, there is nothing at your left knuckles to stop it. To keep the ball from picking up speed, it is possible to move the Cage *up* every time you do the roll. This catches the lateral motion of the ball better than just your knuckles can. After a couple of rolls, you can have the cage at the top of your reach.

Two Fingers: Instead of using the three-finger cradle (see Chapter One), many of my students prefer to use only the first two fingers, spread slightly, to hold and roll the ball (Fig. 4.7). If you use 2" balls or smaller, this may be a better cradle for you. In any case, learning to use the two-finger cradle will help you with the Cage, as well as the next set of tricks.

Figure 4.7
The 2-Finger Cradle

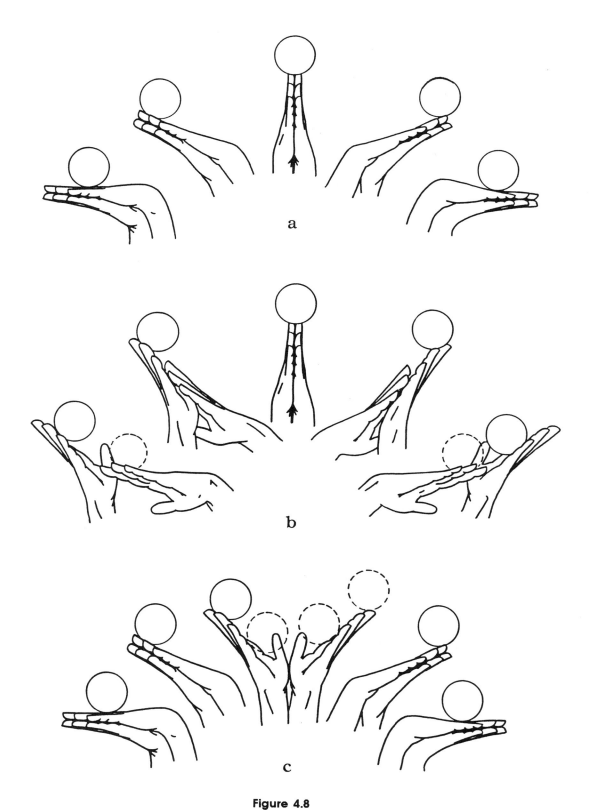

Figure 4.8
Hands-Together Butterfly Variations: (a) Praying Butterfly; (b) Siding in and out; (c) Open in the middle (the "Flytrap"). Note: don't let the dotted balls in (b) confuse you; this illustration was designed to be read in both directions.

Hands Together: Put your palms together, in the first position of the basic Butterfly, as in the leftmost part of Fig. 4.8a. You need to hold the ball in the two-finger cradle, since lowering the middle finger of either hand (or both) is difficult.

Do a Butterfly-type move, keeping your palms together, and catch the ball on the back of the other hand. To learn this, you will have to go through all the basic steps again. This time, to keep your hands from "fighting," you may want to elect a "master" hand. In other words, instead of trying to control each hand separately, and confusing them with redundant information, make one of them dumbly follow the other. This should help to reduce your conscious workload.

Now, from this palms-touching Butterfly (I call it the "praying" Butterfly), you can begin to develop new configurations. If you are exceptionally limber, try a backs-touching Butterfly. Otherwise, learn the next two tricks in Fig. 4.8, and expand from there.

Even More Tricks

The one-ball variations of contact juggling are limitless. It is the responsibility of every juggler to create, discover, and share. The contact juggling moves I have learned or invented thus far are all included, to the best of my ability, in this book. But they are by no means the only ones.

Many moves with billiard balls, which are smaller than the ball I use, are described in a number of very good magic books. Woven in between the productions, vanishes, and multiplications, are a few basic moves of contact juggling.

A lot of magic is done with larger balls, as well. I always enjoy seeing a combined juggling and magic routine, although they usually amount to finishing the cups-and-balls trick by juggling the limes. If you are a magician, try contact juggling your ball before you levitate it!

The concept of contact juggling is not limited to balls, either. There are many moves which are just as elegant in the field of baton twirling, and its cousins: club and torch swinging. I have seen professionals do complex baton work with flame, which ranked with contact juggling in form and complexity. I have also seen a few moves done with plates, knives, and hats, some of which I will cover in Chapter Eight.

And we are not limited to using one ball.

What makes a good juggling trick? For your personal entertainment, and that of other jugglers, obviously the harder tricks will be more impressive. But when entertaining the average audience, we have three types of trick to choose from: those that are exactly as hard as they look, those that look harder than they are, and those that are harder than they look. There are a few, if any, of the ideal case, but most juggling tricks can be said to fall very near it. After all, without a standard to compare with, how are we to say how hard "hard" is? Juggling routines are composed mainly, then, of the first variety of trick: those that are as hard as they look.

Tricks that look harder than they really are include juggling knives, torches, and objects of different weight or size, and the eating of one or more objects as they are being juggled. These are the tricks that pay the juggler. For relatively little practicing, he can reap tremendous benefits, including big tips. The reason for the appeal of these tricks lies actually in their simplicity. The observer can easily describe exactly what he is seeing in words of one or two syllables. He remembers it; he could try it at home.

Those tricks which are harder than they seem, such as juggling seven balls or catching a hat at the end of a balanced pole, are the kind of tricks we learn to impress other jugglers, not the paying public. Seven balls looks fairly hard, but unless you can already do five, it is not as impressive as, say, three bowling balls. That is why most professionals do the big numbers at the beginning of the show, and save the axes and bowling balls for the finale.

There are some tricks that defy this sort of classification. There is, for example, an oriental acrobat who rides a 6' unicycle atop a 4' diameter wooden ball, and while idling up there with one foot, pitches seven bowls from her free leg into another bowl on her head. This trick is, beyond a doubt, even harder than it looks. But I still call it impossible, and so do 99% of the people who see it. That is what makes it a paying trick.

Contact juggling is also, perhaps, even harder than it looks. Still, when executed well, it is worth performing. It's always nice to do a trick they call "impossible."

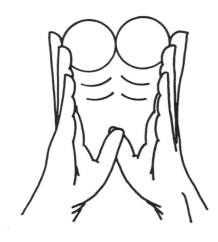

Part Two

Multi-Ball and Beyond

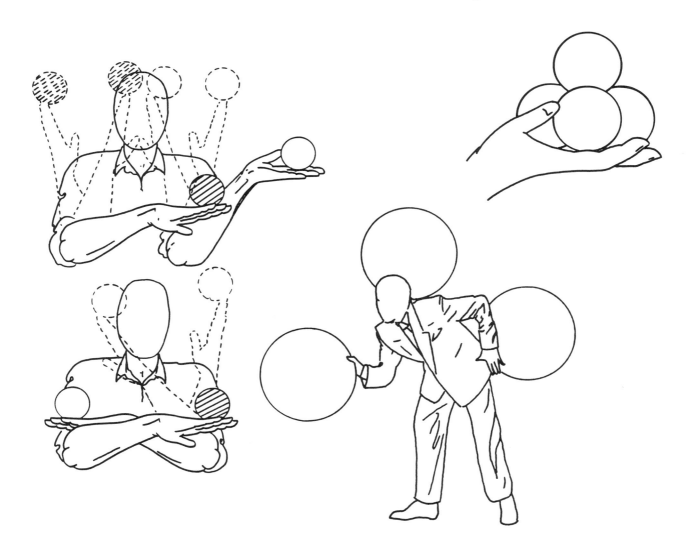

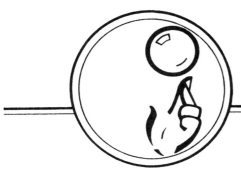

Chapter Five

Two Butterflies & Associated Transfers

There are many logical expansions from one-ball to multi-ball contact juggling. The first group of new tricks includes using a single ball in each hand, and the transfers associated with these moves. The second group (Chapter Six) involves treating several balls as one fluid object, and includes Palm Circles, Stacking, and different transfers. Also included in the second group are tricks which include a ball group in each hand.

The third chapter of this section includes a few multi-ball tricks which do not fit either category, including the Walking Cascade and Three-Ball Staircases.

Extensions and multiplications of the basic Butterfly tend to separate the balls, and are therefore more technical than elegant. It is much harder for an audience to watch two Butterflies at once. Nevertheless, these moves are well worth learning.

If you prefer working with crystal or steel balls, I strongly advise you not to practice these moves with two such balls at once. I prefer to perform the Double Butterfly moves, and any other moves where the balls might collide, with two rubber balls of different colors.

Double Butterflies

Doing a Butterfly in both hands is hard. To learn how, remember to start again at the beginning. Repeat all the steps in Chapter One if you need to, this time with a ball for each hand.

First, pitch a ball and catch it on the back of your right hand, while holding the second ball on the back of your left. Then work the left while the right holds. When you feel comfortable with this, do them both together, or alternate in tempo: right, left, right, left.

Then you're ready for the next step. Go through them all this way.

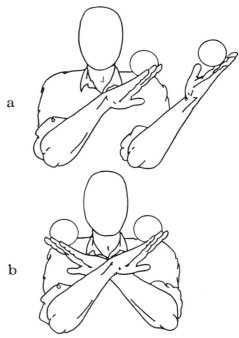

a

b

Figure 5.1
Two Butterflies (a) In tandem; (b)
Crossing in the middle.

Symmetry: When you are doing two Butterflies, you have many options about symmetry. You may want your arms working in tandem (Fig. 5.1a), crossing in the middle (Fig. 5.1b), or going just a little off time. Consider the many ways windshield wipers can be set (or could be if they could cross!).

If your arms are crossing in the middle, be sure to alternate the lead hand, just as you did when learning the basic hand movements.

Another option you have is stalling; that is, holding one hand still for a moment while the other does a half-cycle. This leads to a type of Double Butterfly called "Folding."

•Folding, 1st Variation:

Begin as shown in Fig. 5.2a, with a ball on the back of your right hand, crossing the body, and another on the palm of your left, out in front.

Butterfly the right hand so that it matches the left, as in Fig. 5.2b. Stop.

Now Butterfly the left hand to cross over the right hand (Fig. 5.2c). Stop.

To return to the first position, simply reverse these steps. Blended smoothly, this is one of the simplest and easiest to learn Double Butterflies.

•Folding, 2nd Variation:

This time, begin with arms crossed in front of you, palms down. This is shown in Fig. 5.3a, with the right above the left.

Butterfly the right hand to the outside. Stop. (Fig. 5.3b)

Simultaneously Butterfly the left hand out, and the right hand back in (Fig. 5.3c). Stop.

Butterfly the left hand back down, crossing over the right (Fig. 5.3d).

You are now in the mirror-image of the position where you started. Reverse these moves and you will return to (a).

There are other possible variations of Folding, involving more simultaneous Butterflies as in part 5.3c. Try also maintaining Butterflies in alternate planes, or doing various combinations of one-hand tricks instead of Butterflies (holds, arm rolls, palm spins, etc.).

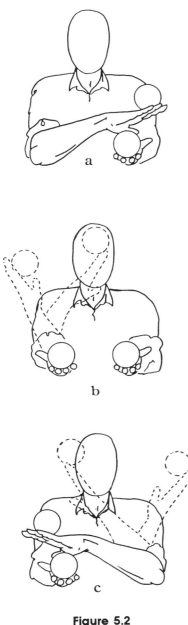

Figure 5.2
Folding, 1st Variation.

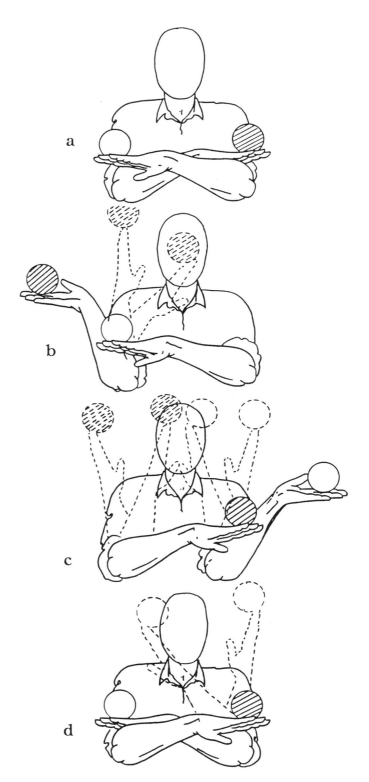

Figure 5.3
Folding, 2nd Variation.

Double Butterfly Transfers

Getting the balls to switch hands is a challenge. Standard Butterfly transfers (those designed for one ball) are of little use to us here, since we cannot roll two balls through the same space at the same time. These two-ball transfers involve putting the extra ball somewhere out of the way, either by holding it, tossing it into the air, or rolling it farther down the arm.

•Back-to-Back With Hold:

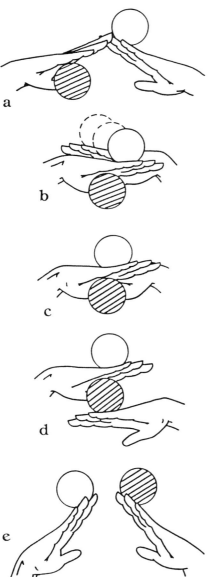

Figure 5.4
Back-to-back with Thumb Hold.

Note: for clarity in describing these transfers, I shall begin with a red ball in the right hand, a white ball in the left.

Do two Butterflies which cross in the middle, as in Fig. 5.1b. When your hands are outside, palm up, grasp the red ball with your right thumb. (See Thumb Hold, Chapter Four). Butterfly the left hand normally.

Now, when you bring your hands to center, they should resemble Fig. 5.4a. Put your right hand in the lead position, for a catch.

Do a Back-to-Back transfer from left to right. The right hand is now holding *both* balls (Fig. 5.4c).

Continue lowering your left hand, while raising your right, and drop the red ball into the left cradle. Now you are free to Butterfly out (Figs. 5.4 d,e).

Another variation of this move is essentially the reverse: Butterfly both hands to center, but hold the right hand above the left. Grab the white ball with the right thumb, then do a Back-to-Back transfer right-to-left (red ball). Butterfly the left out, and grip the white ball on your right palm so that both balls are now on the palms, outside. Resume Double Butterflies.

•Using the Arm:

If you are very good at Arm Rolls (i.e., rolling on the arm above the wrist) try the following transfer. Instead of holding the ball on your right palm to get it "out of the way," you will roll it down towards your elbow.

Figure 5.5a
Using the arm.

In a symmetrical Double Butterfly, bring both hands inside, with the right hand in the lead (Fig. 5.5a).

Roll the red ball down your right arm towards the elbow, and drop the white ball into your right cradle (Fig. 5.5b). Once again, the right "hand" is holding both balls.

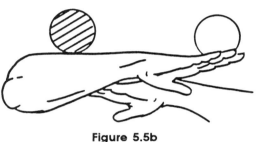

Figure 5.5b

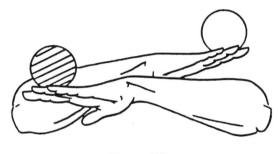

Figure 5.5c

Now bring your left arm under the right, and catch the red ball in the left cradle (Fig. 5.5c).

You are now free to Butterfly both hands back to the outside.

•Using the Air:

Although this type of transfer requires precise timing, I have found it to be the most versatile and appealing. Both the Palm-to-Palm and Back-to-Back variations are easy to learn once you understand them, and they can be combined and repeated in quick succession. This tossing-transfer version of the Circle (Chapter Two) is what I call the Cotton and Water combination.

Since you will do a lot of throwing and catching in these moves, it is almost essential that you know a little three-ball toss juggling. I strongly recommend a short course in three-ball juggling as a preliminary to the tossing transfers. For the basics, see Appendix 2.

•Tossing Palm-to-Palm:

Hold the hands as shown in Fig. 5.6a (to learn these moves, start with empty hands, then try one ball at a time). Butterfly the right hand to the center, as if for a standard Palm-to-Palm transfer.

Toss the white ball into the air (Fig. 5.6b) and roll the red ball from palm to palm. Butterfly the left hand and catch the white ball in the right, ending up as in Fig. 5.6d.

Notice that the white ball does not roll; only the red one. Although it is possible to enter this trick directly from symmetrical Butterflies, I usually prefer to allow the left hand to come to rest beforehand.

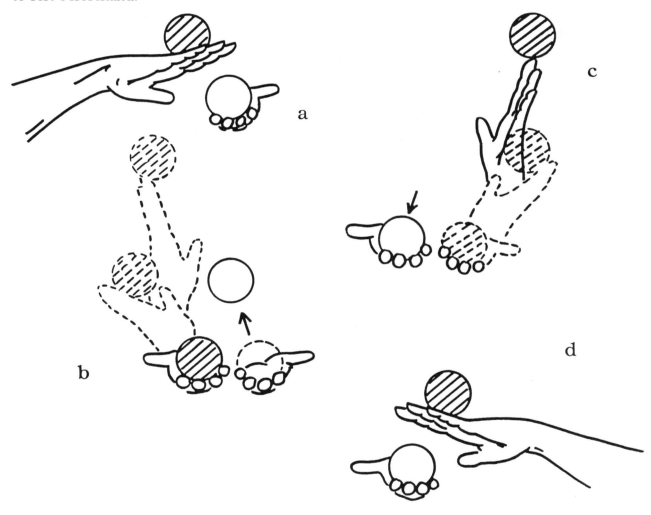

Figure 5.6
Tossing Palm-to-Palm transfer.

•Tossing Back-to-Back:

Begin with the white ball in the left palm. Butterfly the red ball into the right cradle. You should now be in the position shown in Fig. 5.7a.

Toss the white ball into the air, and flip the left hand for a Back-to-Back transfer (Fig 5.7b). Once the red ball has left the right hand, flip that hand and catch the white ball. Butterfly the red ball away on the left hand.

Once again, note that only the white ball is thrown, and only the red ball rolls.

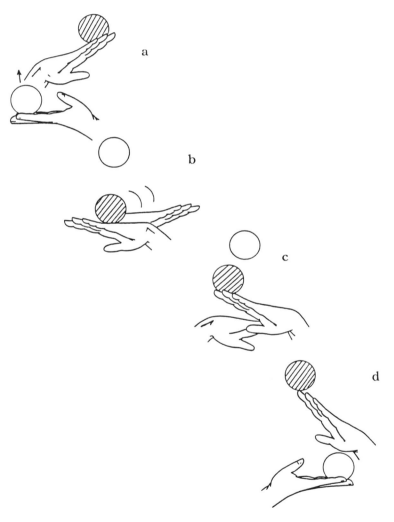

a

b

c

d

Figure 5.7
Tossing Back-to-Back transfer.

•Cotton and Water:

This trick gets its name from a simple phenomenon. If you have a shot glass filled to the rim with water, you might think that nothing else could go into the glass without making it overflow. But you can, in fact, lower several cotton balls into the water without spilling a drop. There is more room in the glass than you thought.

Figure 5.8
Cotton and Water

The basic Circle (Chapter Two) seems as full as the shot glass: both hands are extremely busy repeating the Palm-to-Palm, Back-to-Back combination. However, you can add a tossing transfer to this Circle without slowing it down or "spilling a drop."

In Fig. 5.9 I have depicted a clockwise circle with the white ball, while the red ball is being tossed from hand to hand.

Begin as shown in Fig. 5.9a, and Butterfly the white ball to center for a Palm-to-Palm transfer. Simultaneously throw the red ball into the air.

In Fig. 5.9b, the white ball has rolled under the red ball, into a catch in the right hand (tossing Palm-to-Palm transfer).

Now Butterfly the white ball in the right hand, and toss the red ball back into the air (Fig. 5.9c).

Execute a tossing Back-to-Back, transferring the white ball into the left cradle, and catching the red ball on the right palm. You have now returned to the original position. The white ball has made two circles, and the red ball has been tossed twice.

Although this looks complex, the tossing and catching are almost second nature to an experienced toss juggler. Once again, you must try to invent the simplest variations of this trick to learn it easily. Try it with one real ball and one imagined one, and do the smallest bits of it as separate tricks before stringing them together.

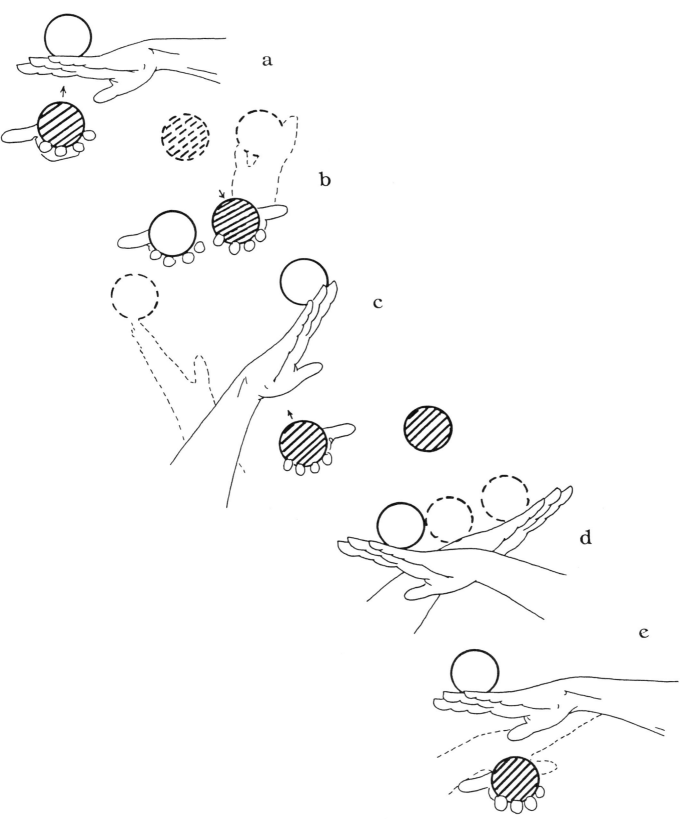

Figure 5.9
The Cotton and Water tossing-transfer combination.

There are many variations on these Double Butterfly transfers, in each of the holding, rolling, and tossing categories. Do your best to invent subtly different ones: try some in different Butterfly planes, or while Folding. Try especially the holding and tossing variations of Palm-to-Back and Back-to-Palm transfers. They are quite simple alterations of the ones I have described.

One of them (I call it the P.B.&J.) involves repeated Palm-to-Back transfers, with a toss ("jump") from the back of the catching hand to the palm of the throwing hand. The crucial moments of this, as well as its brother the B.P.&J., are shown in Fig. 5.10.

In addition to the multi-ball transfers, there are other obvious expansions of the Butterfly, many with the word "while" in them. For example, you might keep a Butterfly going in your right hand while you:

(a) Juggle two in the left hand　　(b) Balance on one foot

(c) Sing　　(d) Balance a pole on your nose

(And don't forget "All of the above.")

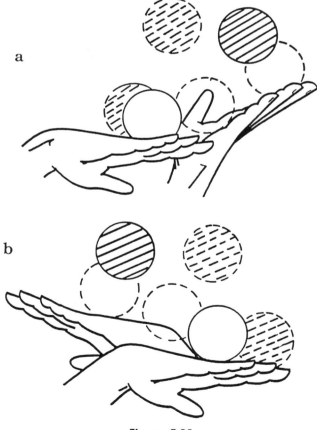

Figure 5.10
Two more tossing transfers.

Chapter Six
Palm Circles

The second large group of multiple-ball tricks is Palm Circling, or Palm Spinning. This is as mesmerizing and as difficult as single-ball work, and can be the basis for an entire routine.

The materials for Palm Circles are slightly different. The balls you use may be smaller than for single-ball (especially at first, or if you have small hands). New rubber balls are sticky and will catch on each other when they rub together. Older balls (especially lacrosse) will get slicker as the rubber ages. Steel Chinese exercise balls are excellent for Palm Circles, since they are smaller and smoother. They are, however, expensive, especially if you want to use four pairs. If you use crystal or lucite balls, you may find it useful to polish the balls with a transparent lubricant, since these surfaces grab each other when dry.

Two Balls

Hold your arm comfortably low, with your palms up and forearms level, as if you were carrying a tray. This plane is called the "tray" plane. Put two balls on your palm, and push them around in a circle.

You should be pushing with your fingers and thumb. (I once met someone who, I kid you not, thought he wasn't "allowed" to use his thumb. This may be true in some kind of martial art, but not in contact juggling). It would help the spinning to tilt your hand forward a little, but try not to do this. If you rely on a forward tilt, you will never be able to do a stack of four balls. Instead, stay in the tray plane.

Figure 6.1
Two balls

A few factors to consider: traditionally, Chinese exercise balls are not supposed to touch during this move. This is okay for two balls, but bad for three and impossible for four. Work, for the moment, on both styles. When you're holding them together, keep them in constant contact with centripetal pressure. When keeping them apart, make sure they never touch. Keeping the balls apart is the only way to do tacky rubber.

You may also choose between clockwise and counterclockwise motion. You should notice that, just as you have a good and bad hand, you also have an easy and hard direction of spin. My hardest spin is counterclockwise on my left hand. Once again, work them all.

Three Balls

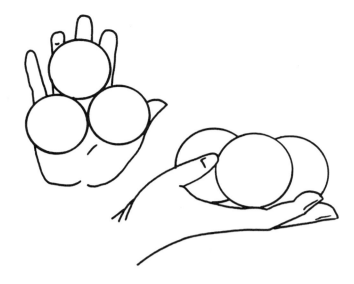

Figure 6.2
Three balls

Once you have become comfortable with all the variations of two balls, add a third one. It will feel huge, at first. That's okay; once you can do three, two will feel small. Juggling works that way.

Forget about keeping the balls apart. Push them together with as much control as you can, and keep them going at a constant speed. Thumb and pinkie are the principal movers with three balls.

Work on increasing your speed, smoothness in both directions, changing directions, and using both hands at once. The biggest problem with palm spinning is inconsistent speed. The circle will tend to lurch forward when you have a good grip on it, and stop dead where you can't push it.

Listen for little clicks when the balls separate and hit each other again. This means you aren't holding them together, and you'll never hold up ball number four.

Four Balls

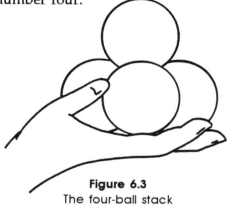

Figure 6.3
The four-ball stack

When you are able to keep three balls spinning on your palm, it is time to add ball number four. Set it on top. Here's where level palm and steady pressure pay off: if you can keep three balls together well enough, the fourth will ride easily on top of the stack. You will feel a little extra pressure forcing the circle apart, but other than that, the four-ball stack is essentially the same as three.

You might notice that the top ball spins very fast. This is a result of the configuration—the place where the ball is contacting the others. It's like a gear reduction that makes the top ball spin about three times as fast as the others.

Of course, if you're using solid colors, no one will see it spinning but you. Try adding a second color to the ball, or put a striped or spotted ball on top. The effect is unusual.

Cascade: When using small enough balls, you can get them to move in a cascade (figure-eight) by breaking them into two smaller circles (Fig. 6.4 a-f). Unless you have superb control, the balls tend to slam together when the larger circle reforms, but experiment with it. Try a cascade or a reverse cascade in this manner. Along with two directions of circles, you can make some complicated combinations.

Breaking the Tray Plane: This is easiest with three balls. Orient the balls so that one is out on your fingertips, the other two back on your palm (Fig. 6.5a). Instead of rolling the ball around or between the others, push it up and over (Fig. 6.5b). Now continue spinning.

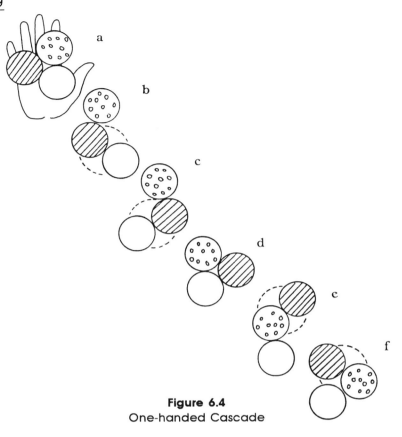

Figure 6.4
One-handed Cascade

You might also push a ball up and over with your pinkie (Fig. 6.5c) or with your thumb (Fig. 6.5d). Combine these in quick succession and it starts to look like three bubbles blowing in the wind.

There are also variations of this using a four-ball stack. You are basically just turning the faces of the pyramid (Fig. 6.5 e,f).

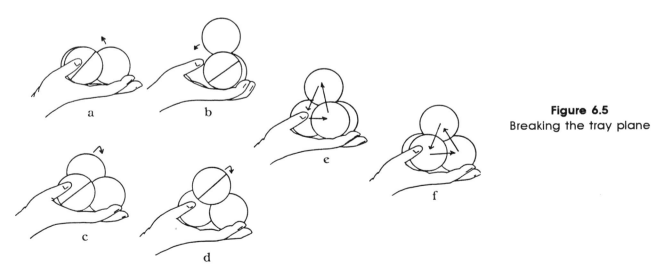

Figure 6.5
Breaking the tray plane

Inverting: If you are using smaller balls, you might be able to hold two or three balls (but probably not four!) upside down and continue spinning them. In the case of a pair of steel exercise balls, this is actually one of the recommended exercises. If you can invert them, you can also rotate the tray plane to any orientation (Fig. 6.6 a,b).

Leaving the Palm: While doing a four-ball stack, roll the top ball up your arm to the elbow and hold it there. Continue spinning the three on your palm. Now, gently roll the fourth ball back down and onto the top of the stack. This is one of those moves which (for me) happened first by accident (Fig. 6.7).

You may find it easier to roll one of the balls off the bottom and simultaneously drop the top ball down to replace it. You can also reverse this process when you put it back.

Now, do a two-ball Palm Circle. Grip one of the balls with your thumb, and Butterfly the other into the cradle (Fig. 6.8 a-c). From here you may want to return to Palm Spinning, or go into some Butterfly variations.

If you are able to spin two or three balls inverted, you may want to try a similar move with three or four balls. Roll one of the balls to the back of your hand, and keep the others spinning upside down. In this case, you must use the two-finger cradle, or hold the ball on the smooth part of the back of your hand.

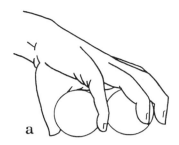
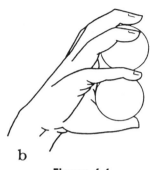

Figure 6.6
Gripping the spin: (a) inverted; (b) vertical.

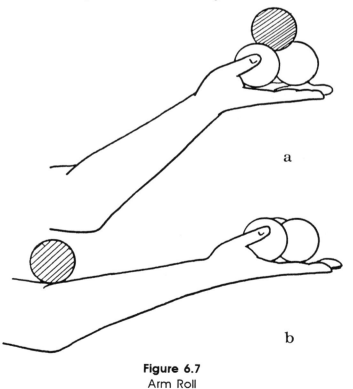

Figure 6.7
Arm Roll

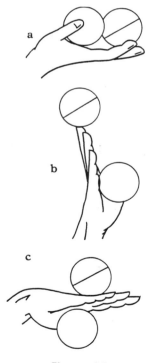

Figure 6.8
Butterfly into Thumb Hold

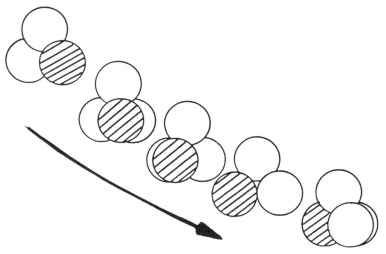

Figure 6.9
Lateral
Movement

Lateral Movement: Simply moving a stack of balls slowly sideways gives it a new look. Try skimming three or four balls close to the ground like a flying saucer. (Trust me on this one.)

Palm Spinning in Two Hands: Transfers, Larger Groups, and Curls

If you can maintain a four-ball stack in either hand, doing both hands at once is not really that hard. Your hands, not your eyes, do most of the work, which actually leaves your

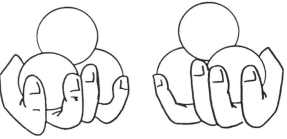

Figure 6.10
Both hands at once.

eyes (and head) free for another trick—balancing, mouth juggling, head rolls, etc.

Apart from doing spins in each hand, there are many spinning moves which involve both hands working together.

Transfers: If you keep your hands flat, palm up, and in the tray plane, you can transfer palm spins from one hand to the other.

You might send a clockwise spin from right to left, or change directions as you change hands. When moving three balls from hand to hand, it is good to pick a lead ball and let the others trail off after it. This also works with four.

Try spinning three balls on both hands together; that is, with your hands

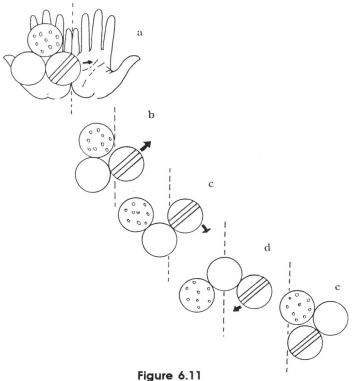

Figure 6.11
Changing directions while changing hands (notice the path of the leading ball).

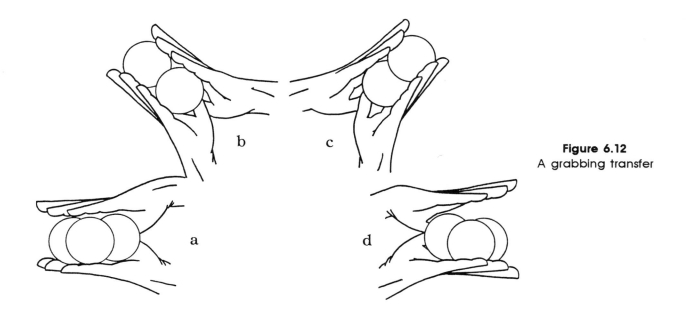

Figure 6.12
A grabbing transfer

b   c

a   d

next to each other. Do a circle or cascade with three balls. You can actually cascade up to seven large balls in this manner, without even breaking the tray plane.

Now, try breaking the tray plane.

Grabbing: If you can do inverted palm spins (Fig. 6.6) you may want to just grab a three-ball spin off of one hand with the other. If you can't do inverted palm spins, you can still do a grabbing transfer.

Grabbing two or three: As in Fig. 6.12, let the grabbing hand be helped by the other until it is under the balls. In other words, hold the group with both hands during the transfer.

You might try some out-of-plane moves while in positions (b) and (c).

Grabbing four: This is similar to grabbing two or three, but you must approach the pyramid from one of its faces, rather than from the top.

The four-ball grab lends itself to a lot of plane-breaking in the middle phase (Fig. 6.13). Try holding your hands together and rotating the three balls in the top plane. Bigger balls are better for this trick, because smaller ones get lost behind your fingers.

Figure 6.13
Plane breaking in the 4-ball grab.

•Curls:

An expansion of lateral movement is curling (Fig. 6.14). This is adapted from a dancing move done mostly with plates or candles. The object is to move your hands in a complete circle below, and then above, your shoulder.

a

b

c

d

e

f

g

Figure 6.14
A one-handed Curl

Practice first with a plate, and then with a group of balls which are not spinning, before trying a spinning stack.

Begin by bringing your hand under your armpit, with the elbow out. As you bring your hand further around, push your shoulder forward and straighten your arm, until it is twisted almost to the maximum (Fig. 6.14, a-c).

Now, untwist your arm, lifting your hand up above shoulder level. Make another circle , and bring your hand back down to where it began (Fig. 6.14, d-g).

Practice this move with both arms alternating. When one side is up, the other should be down. It is also possible to do both sides symmetrically, but this is harder and requires a limber back.

I suppose that continuous alternating curls with a four-ball stack on each hand is the most complicated ball spinning trick I have seen. If you can do this, consider yourself an accomplished palm spinner.

Figure 6.15
Simultaneous Curls

Other Variations

Remember that even if you can spin four balls on each hand, two balls is still a nice trick. Experiment with different numbers on each hand, moving two spins relative to each other, and transferring only parts of stacks (for example, splitting a four-ball stack into two spinning pairs).

The very act of adding and removing balls can be mesmerizing when executed properly.

If you can do Inverted Stacks, try this: Hold a seventh ball between two vertical triplets. The hands-together variations of plane-breaking would also be interesting.

Above all, remember to experiment. Sometimes it is impossible to visualize a new trick until you do it.

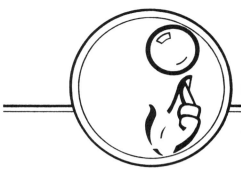

Chapter Seven

A Few Other Multi-Ball Tricks

Walking Cascade

If you can do the Side Stepping version of walking with one ball (Chapter Three), it is easy to learn the Walking Cascades.

First Version: You need to learn two separate holds on the palm of each hand. One is out near the fingertips, and the other is the thumb hold against the palm (Fig. 7.1). Begin with the balls as shown in Fig. 7.2a, with a ball on the fingers of each hand, and a third held by the right thumb.

Figure 7.1
Thumb Hold for the Walking Cascade.

Turn your right hand towards the left, and roll the ball from the right fingertips to the left thumb hold (Fig. 7.2b).

Now, as you turn the left hand towards the right, roll the blue ball from the right thumb hold to the right fingertips. You are now in the reverse position from where you began, with the left hand poised to roll the red ball into the right thumb hold (Fig. 7.2 c,d).

To stretch the first version, start releasing the balls further up the arm,

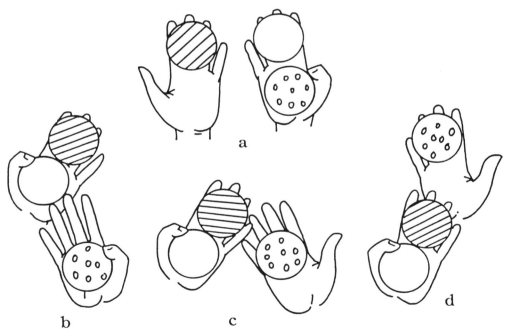

Figure 7.2
Walking Cascade, from above (see also Fig. 3.4).

and rolling them into the thumb hold.

Second Version: You can also do this cascade walking towards yourself instead of away. The moves are basically reversed, and to stretch it just use more of the forearm before dropping the ball to the fingertips.

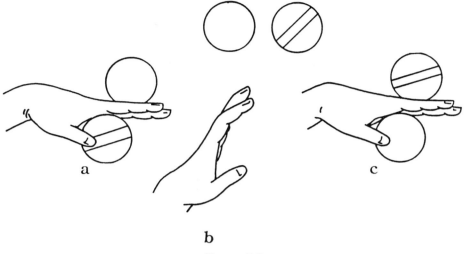

Toss and Grab

This is one of the most well known two-ball tricks. Hold a red ball against your right palm, palm down. Put a white ball in the cradle of the same hand (the two-finger cradle works well for this) as in Fig. 7.3a.

Throw both balls up, not more than a foot. Grab the white ball first, before the red one begins to fall, against your palm, and then catch the red ball in the cradle.

Figure 7.3
The Toss-and-Grab Exchange.

The balls have traded places.

There are also variations of this type of move using three and four balls (in two hands).

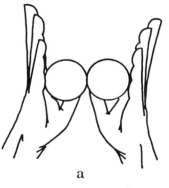

(Two-Ball) Elevator

This is a fairly self-explanatory trick. Simply hold the two balls as shown in Fig. 7.4, raising and lowering them. You might also try inverting the hands, as in the Mineshaft (Chapter Four), or rolling the pair down between your forearms. Once the balls leave your palms this becomes a *much* harder trick.

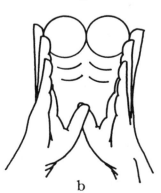

Three-Ball Staircases

Many variations of basic Butterfly transfers can be done with three balls. The ones I will describe involve thumb holds, much like

Figure 7.4
The (2-Ball) Elevator.

the Walking Cascade. In fact, that was a simple example of the Three-Ball Butterfly transfers which are possible. The next simple example is the (Three-Ball) Descending Staircase.

Descending Staircases: Hold a ball against each palm while doing a Descending Staircase (Fig 7.5). That's about it. You might also try walking the ball on the backs of your hands, either way, towards you, or side-to-side.

Adding a Butterfly: Now, put a Butterfly into the pattern. Begin with the hands and balls as shown in Fig. 7.6a. Set the white ball in the left cradle, and Butterfly the red ball in the right hand, out and back. Then grab the white ball again and resume the Descending Staircase (Fig. 7.6 b,c).

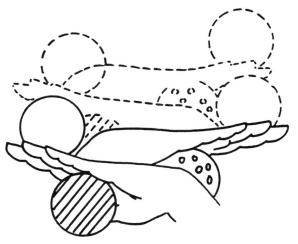

Figure 7.5
3-Ball Descending Staircase.

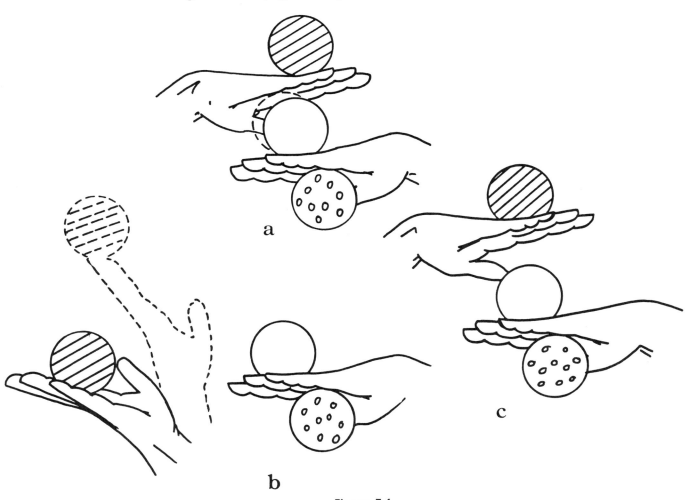

Figure 7.6
Adding a Butterfly.

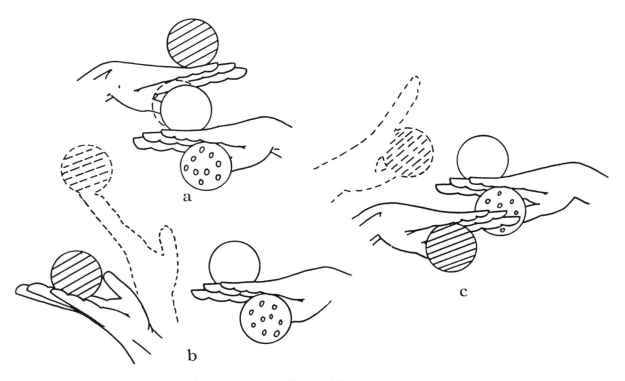

Figure 7.7
Getting Complex.

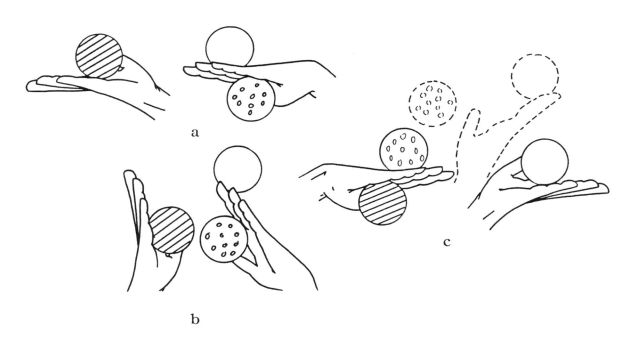

Figure 7.8
Simultaneous Dropping.

Getting Complex: Now, do the right-handed Butterfly, just as you did before, but only halfway. This puts you in the position in Fig. 7.7b. This time, when you return, grip the ball instead of rolling it, and go right back into the Descending Staircase, now with the white ball on top.

Simultaneous Dropping: The next step is a big one. Begin again as shown in Fig. 7.6a, but this time Butterfly the right hand first, and as you do it, drop the white ball into the left cradle. You should end up as in Fig. 7.8a.

To repeat this move on the other side, you must do the following three things: Grip the red ball against your right palm, Butterfly the white ball in the left, and drop the blue ball into a catch on the right cradle (Fig. 7.8 a-c). Now repeat the sequence in reverse order to return to where you started.

From this move there are a great variety of variations, involving various holds, transfers, and different planes. Experiment.

Remember also to try other backs-only moves while gripping the ball on your palms. The Cage, a Twisting Butterfly (on the back), and even toss juggling (on the backs) could be done in this manner.

Chapter Eight

Other Objects and Ideas

Although balls are the most versatile shape for juggling, other objects do lend themselves to a few contact juggling moves. I have seen limited routines done with plates, hats, sticks, knives, coins, and cards.

I have also seen wonderful adaptations of contact juggling involving other art forms, including magic, dance, gymnastics, and the martial arts.

Also included here are some tricks which involve replacing the hands with other items, including ball-on-plate, ball-on-ball, and Devil Sticks.

Most of the moves which are possible with other objects have already been discussed in other books, and so for more details on them I refer you to my suggested reading list on page 93.

Plates

One of the most elegant moves I have seen with other objects is Plate Flipping. Start with a plate on your left hand (I use an 18" serving tray. You might also try a china plate or a stiff hat). Bring the right hand up behind it, palm down, as in the first part of Fig. 8.1.

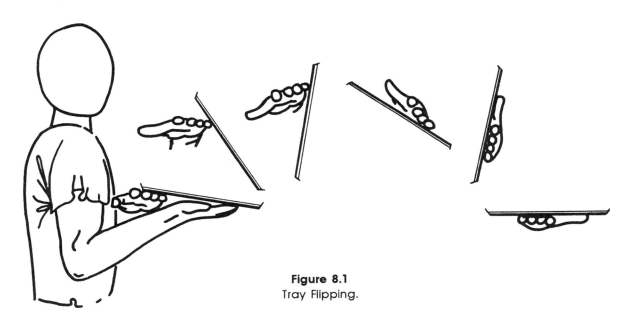

Figure 8.1
Tray Flipping.

Lift the plate with the edge of your right hand and turn it for a whole flip, to be caught on your right palm.

If you turn your left hand palm down during this flip, you can set yourself up to repeat the trick on the other side.

Try doing the same sort of move pulling the plate in towards yourself. You can also do this move with one hand by giving the plate a little toss, and then coming up under it with the same hand.

Curls (Chapter Six) can also be done with plates. Try setting a wineglass or candle on the plate before you curl it.

Centripetal Swings: If you do it quickly and smoothly, you can swing a plate upside down over your head, through a full circle and back without dropping it. Try this in various planes and through various curves. If you feel confident, try swinging a glass-on-plate stack (do it first with something that won't break!).

Figure 8.2
Back Rolls with plates or hoops,
from a photo of Bob Bramson.

Plates also lend themselves to body rolls, especially Arm and Back Rolls (Figure 8.2). Any roll which does not stop the plate and reverse its direction will work (i.e., Butterflies and Head Rolls are tough). You might also try rolling hoops or hats. Some hats can be rolled on the rim or end-over-end.

Other platelike objects include books, frisbees, and cigar boxes. Experiment with various objects to see which manipulations work best.

Sticks and "Knives"

The most common form of contact juggling with sticks is called baton twirling. Twirling batons typically measure about 25" to 30" in length, with slender midsections and weighted knobs at both ends. These knobs make the baton easier to catch, increase its moment of inertia (a property related to angular momentum), and are often solid enough to make the baton bounce off hard surfaces.

Single baton work is basically of two varieties: contact juggling ("twirling") and toss juggling ("release moves"). The contact juggling tricks include finger rolls, figure-eights, and body rolls with the arms, legs, body, neck, and head. Wrap-around body rolls (such as the back- and neck-rolls) are even easier with longer sticks.

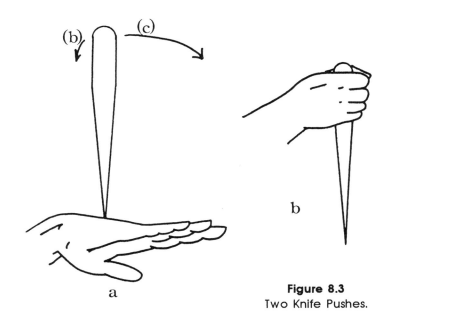

Figure 8.3
Two Knife Pushes.

a

b

c

I have seen a couple of nice moves with knives which I will explain. By "knife," I mean a short stick with more weight at the handle than at the other end. I happen to perform with daggers of various lengths, but this is only because I am very confident of my ability. Practice with appropriately sized dowels, and don't be ashamed to perform with them, too.

The first knife move is a "push," done best with a tapered stick about 6-8 inches long. Start with the stick balanced point-down on the back of your hand, in the inside position of the basic Butterfly (Fig. 8.3a). If it's a knife, it had better be light and dull! Now, either:

- Roll the stick away from yourself, over the edge of your hand, and catch it point-down as in Fig 8.3b, or

- Butterfly the stick over your fingertips and catch it as in Fig. 8.3c.

These pushes can also be done with pencils, screwdrivers, pingpong paddles, etc.

The second knife move is a palm spin, and it is best done with a 12"-16" knife (or tapered stick). Hold the knife with its center of balance on your palm. Your hand should be out in front of you, palm up. Give the knife a quick clockwise spin (counterclockwise for the left hand) and flatten your hand out to let the blade pass.

Stop it again when the knife has completed a full circle (Fig. 8.4). This is sort of the 16th century version of the gunslinger's twirl.

You obviously don't need a knife to do this trick. A short stick is fine to practice with—try a juggling club, flashlight, or the bottom

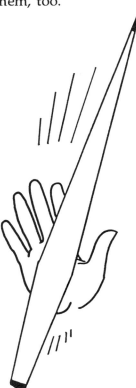

Figure 8.4
Palm Spinning
a short stick.

half of a pool cue. And once you can do a single spin, try letting it continue for a second, third, or fourth spin.

Coins and Cards

Most magic books cover a multitude of tricks done with coins and cards including fanning, cutting and shuffling, finger rolling, and one-handed vanishes and productions. The moves with cards usually tend to treat the deck as a single fluid object, or sometimes two.

Magicians seem to have won custody of these tricks, because they blend well with many illusions which are possible with the same props. But there is no reason why even an "honest" juggler could not perform them.

Working in the Other Arts

One of the best ways to advance an art form is to merge it with another. Many magicians could learn contact juggling to insert in a ball routine—either levitating, vanishing, or fortune telling. Many contact Jugglers perform as much dance as juggling, choreographing brilliant routines to music. Dancers, too, do some juggling in their routines. For a great example, watch Fred Astaire dance with a coat rack in *Royal Wedding*.

One of my students is incorporating contact juggling in his Tai Chi exercises. He goes through the basic body positions while holding and rolling balls. Examining the martial art has given him tremendous insight into the possibilities of contact juggling, and practicing with the balls has improved his skill at Tai Chi.

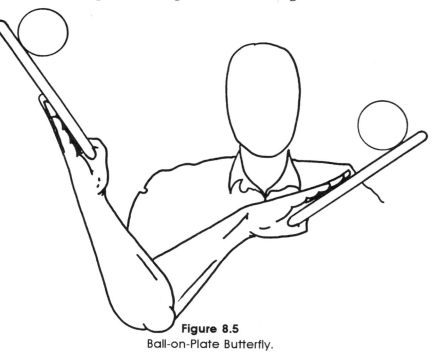

Replacing the Hands

Contact juggling (with balls) can be done not only on the hands and body, but also on a multitude of replacements: plates, sticks, balls, etc. Stick-on-stick juggling is better known as Devil Sticks (see Appendix II for a short lesson).

Figure 8.5
Ball-on-Plate Butterfly.

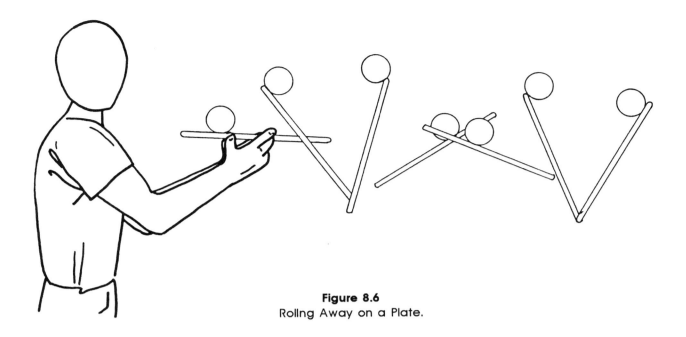

Figure 8.6
Rolling Away on a Plate.

Plates: If your plate is perfectly flat on both sides, you should be able to do the Butterfly on it (Fig. 8.5). Try cutting a small circle or rectangle out of plywood and using it as an extension of your hand. I prefer a small, circular cutting board, which I can also flip and roll with one hand. For ball-on-plate work, use the tackiest (best grip) ball you can find.

With a larger plate, it is also possible to do a continuous roll: turning the plate end-over-end while the ball rolls over it, much like an ant trying to stay on top of your hand (Fig. 8.6).

The same effect is possible (and much easier) with two large balls. I like to use beach balls for this one. Hold and turn the lower ball, while the other rolls along the top (Fig. 8.7). A similar trick can be done with a ball on an umbrella.

I have discovered that the best way to design tricks with new items is to buy or build the item I need, and then to experiment with it. It is hard to imagine how a particular trick will work until you actually try it. You cannot devise the perfect prop until you have worked with several imperfect ones, and you will never stumble upon a new idea with imaginary toys. As I write this I am sitting at my desk and wondering about the possibilities of Ball-on-Telephone....

Figure 8.7
Ball-on-Ball.

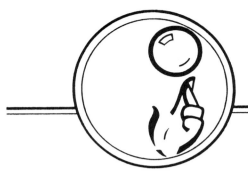

Appendix I
Materials

Following is a brief description of the best props to use for practicing and performing contact juggling.

Figure A.1
Balls

Balls

Contact juggling is fluid and graceful, and whatever ball you choose should seem to float. Solid colors, completely reflective balls, and crystal balls are ideal for this illusion. But these may not be suitable for practice. Nice white balls crack and stain, metal balls dull and dent, and crystal balls chip.

Practice with a ball that is similar to your performance ball in size and weight; appearance doesn't matter much. Your practice balls should be inexpensive, fairly heavy, and rugged. They should also be safe for things they might hit: furniture, the cat, each other, or you.

For single-ball tricks, rubber balls work well. New lacrosse balls have a decent grip and a good weight. Another good practice ball is a Hartz (or similar) dog ball, made of solid rubber. These balls are a little more dense than lacrosse balls, and might be easier to come by. If you have a dog, it may be hard to keep him away from your practice ball, so find a safe place to keep it.

Various balls are available from juggling suppliers. Look for a ball about medium sized ($2^1/_2$"-3"), and fairly heavy (six ounces or more). Silicone balls, the newest thing in juggling balls, are absolutely perfect for one-ball work, but they will run upwards of $25 apiece.

Try to avoid lighter balls, which tend to move in jerky patterns and fly away when you make mistakes. Pick a ball that is visually about as big as your hand; larger balls tend to hide the hands, while smaller ones are hidden. For body rolls, larger balls are ideal, so try volleyballs, basketballs, beach balls, etc.

If you want to work with crystal or lucite balls, they can be difficult to find. A small number of juggling suppliers have begun carrying lucite balls, and you might place a call to a local plastics company to get some ideas. Lucite balls vary wildly in price, from five to thirty dollars apiece in the $2^1/_2$" size, depending on quality, supply, and demand.

Shops that specialize in crystal glassware, suncatchers, pewter figurines and things of that ilk may carry crystal balls. If they do not have any in stock, you might be able to order them through the catalogs they use, if you can get chummy with the manager. Expect to pay $35-$55 or more for a $2^1/_2$" (65mm) crystal ball; much more if you go any larger.

Multiple Balls

2" balls (and smaller) are suited to multi-ball work, but the bigger you can go, the better. If you use rubber balls, you may want to lubricate them or simply let the rubber get slick with age. (Warning: Silicone Balls *don't* age!)

Steel Chinese exercise balls, the kind with the chimes in them, are good for multi-ball work, and provide their own background music. I have seen them vary in size from 2" to less than an inch, and they can be very expensive. As with anything else in low demand, these items will vary wildly in price from place to place. Check for them at import stores, yuppie junk stores (your worst price, I guarantee), and martial arts equipment retailers/wholesalers. Be sure to measure them before you buy them, too. They aren't standardized.

Crystal balls in the 2" range are often available in different colors. You can expect to pay around $20-$25 apiece for these, so if you plan on performing with eight balls, you'd better be very certain about the color(s) you pick! Of course, if you're looking for a completely new effect and money is no object (you're learning to juggle because the yacht got dull) pick your eight favorite semi-precious stones and get a $2^1/_4$" sphere made of each one. Seriously, obsidian, malachite, and other stones make pretty balls, but don't ever expect to find two the same size.

Other Items

Juggling suppliers carry other props, but I prefer to make my own, or buy ordinary items. Anyone who has a minimum of shop tools (or a friend with same) can save money making his own plates, Devil Sticks, clubs, etc. You can also design and redesign the perfect prop for your newest trick. For example, the "spinning plates" sold in juggling catalogs are totally useless for the moves I perform (even the spinning ones). I prefer an unaltered or center-drilled 18" fiberglass serving tray, or a circle cut from $1/_2$" or $1/_4$" plywood. Cards, coins, and sporting equipment are available anywhere, and seldom require any sort of modification.

Appendix II

The Three-Ball Cascade & Walking Devil Sticks

Because I have recommended that non-jugglers learn at least one other style as they work through this book, I have provided here a basic lesson in a couple of these styles. For a more thorough expansion of these and other basic tricks, I refer you to my list of suggested reading.

The Three-Ball Cascade

The simplest pattern in which to toss juggle three balls is a horizontal figure-eight called the Cascade (Fig. A.2). To learn this, build up to it slowly, practicing simpler versions of the final goal.

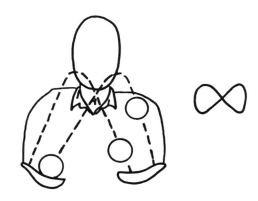

Figure A.2
The Figure-Eight "Cascade."

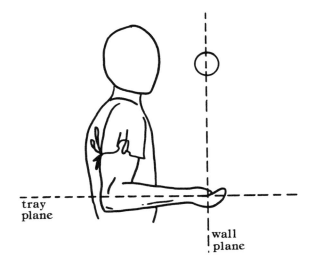

Figure A.3
Tray & Wall Planes for the 3-Ball Cascade.

Hand Position: Hold your arms as shown in Fig. A.3, shoulders relaxed, with your forearms level, as if you were carrying a tray of water glasses. You don't want to reach very far above or below this tray plane when juggling three balls. (Don't spill the water.)

The balls will be travelling in a vertical plane, called the wall plane, above your hands. If you keep your hands within this plane, the balls should stay there, too.

To warm up in this space, try moving your hands in little circles in the wall plane. Don't move them symmetrically; alternate left-right-left-right, since this is the way they will work in the Cascade. For the moment, bring them up on the inside, down on the outside, as in Fig. A.4.

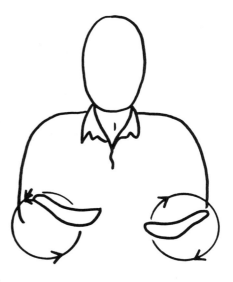

Figure A.4
Little Circles

•One Ball

Now begin tossing the ball from hand to hand, within the wall plane. The ball should go up to about eye level. Eye level throws are a good compromise between low throws (not enough time) and high ones (not enough control). Notice right away if you have a tendency to throw too far forward (away from yourself) or backward, and correct that habit as best you can in the one-ball phase. I have found that the best way to fix a forward throw is to learn to throw too far *back*, and then compromise between the two.

If you begin moving your hands in the circles described in Fig. A.4, you will develop two separate arches: one right-to-left arch, and the other left-to-right (Fig. A.5, a&b). These are the two arches which will compose the Cascade. (If both hands threw in the same arch, the balls would collide.)

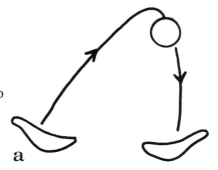

a

•Two-Ball Exchange

Start with a ball in each hand (red in right, white in left). Throw the red ball first, and when it is on its way down (Fig A.6b), throw the white one back. Your first impulse may be to quickly hand it over to the right hand instead of throwing it. Try to break this habit: it works with two, but it won't be easy with three. Imagine in your mind the rhythm: throw-throw-catch-catch.

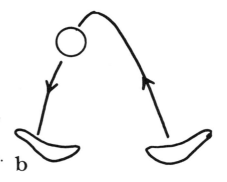

b

Figure A.5
One Ball.
Note: In an effort to simplify these illustrations, I have represented the hands as though they were stationary. This has the side effect of bending the paths traced through the air. Be assured that juggling balls travel in simple parabolas like any other projectiles.

Learn this exchange in both directions. The first ball you throw is called the "lead" throw, and the second is the "response" throw. Since the balls change hands each time, if you throw the red ball first each time, you will work both directions evenly.

If you had only a small problem with your control of one ball, it may show up in your exchange of two. Notice if you have to move your hands significantly out of the tray or wall

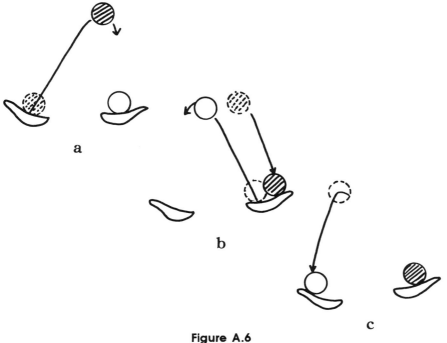

Figure A.6
The Two-Ball Exchange.

a

plane to make a catch. Any small errors you make now will grow much worse with three balls—and they are easier to correct by working on only two.

Also make sure that both throws are going the same height. They are, for purposes of the three-ball Cascade, mirrored copies of the same throw.

•Stowaway

To learn to start and stop three balls, you first need to learn to hold a stowaway—that is, a second ball held by the last two fingers against the palm. Learn to throw and catch a ball using only the thumb and first two fingers, while you hold the stowaway (Fig. A.7).

b

Figure A.7
The Stowaway.

•Three Balls

To juggle three balls, begin as you did before: Throw the first ball from the hand which holds two. As it falls, throw the first response. The first response (second throw) becomes the lead ball for the third throw, which in turn is the lead ball for the fourth throw. You are basically just repeating the two-ball exchange indefinitely (Fig. A.8).

If you have trouble doing this on your first try (most people do) try simpler versions. Try three throws and stop. If you can't catch them all, just throw them away, 1-2-3. Watch where they go. If they travel in the right paths, you can start catching them.

After three throws and three catches becomes easy, move on to four and four. Then five throws, then ten. Once you can get to 100 throws, you can stop counting.

Some simple variations of toss juggling are depicted in Fig. A.9.

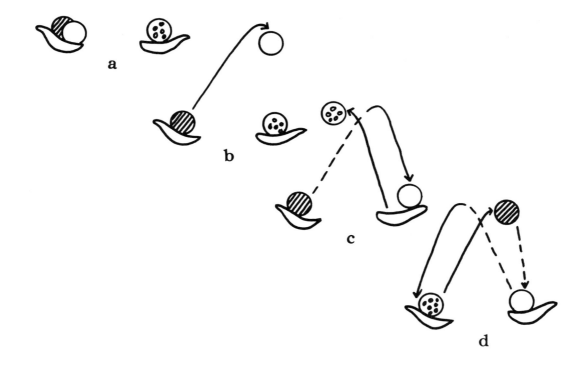

Figure A.8
The first few throws of the 3-Ball Cascade.

Figure A.9
(a) Two in one hand, Outside Circles; (b) Inside Circles; (c) "Parallel"; (d) 3-Ball Cascade; (e) Reverse Cascade (up on the outside, down on the inside); (f) Half-Reverse Cascade.

•Walking Devil Sticks

If you'd like to make your own Devil Sticks, I would recommend a 28" x 1¹/₂" dowel, shaved (with a draw knife or a lathe) to less than ³/₄" in the center. Wrap it with fake suede leather (the stickier the better) or bicycle handgrip tape. For the two handsticks use 14" x ¹/₂" dowels, covered in ¹/₂" inside diameter black surgical tubing. Keep the leather clean and wash the rubber tubing with acetone to make it grip as well as possible. Mark the center of the baton (long stick) with white tape.

The baton can also be replaced by a tennis racket. I prefer the wooden kind, which usually have straighter handles and a little more weight. The only disadvantage to using a tennis racket is that you can only strike one end, but for the basic walk that's just fine.

The basic "tic-toc," or walk, with Devil Sticks involves keeping the baton aloft by tapping it with the handsticks, left-right-left-right. Both sticks push up and to the inside, the resultant push being straight up.

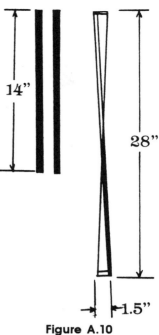

Figure A.10
Devil Stick Dimensions.

To get used to the way this should feel, try walking the baton on your hands first (Figure A.11). Grip it about halfway between the center and one end. This is the contact point for the basic walk. To get more lift with less spin, hit it closer to the center; for less lift and more spin, hit it near the end.

Walk the baton slowly in your hands, left-right-left-right, laying it all the way to the horizontal each time. The slower you go, the easier it will be. Notice that you don't need to grip the baton; you can simply support it at the proper point.

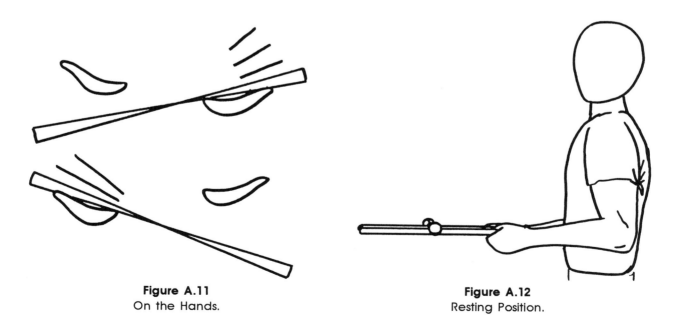

Figure A.11
On the Hands.

Figure A.12
Resting Position.

Now, pick up the handsticks. To get used to the weight of the baton on the sticks, just hold it there, or roll it out to the ends of the handsticks and back. Throw it up with no spin, and catch it again.

Now throw the baton for a half-flip. The ideal way to do this is to let one hand do all of the throwing work, while the other does all the catching. For example, to throw a half-flip from right to left, start with the baton horizontal (Fig. A.13a). Drop the left handstick out of the way and push up with the right. This imparts the lift and the spin (Fig. A.13b). To stop the spin and the fall, bring the left handstick up under the contact point and gently catch the baton (Fig. A.13d). Once it is horizontal, bring the right up for support.

Now try a return (two half-flips in series). Start level, throw a half-flip right-to-left, and then without using the right handstick to stop it, throw the stick back for another half-flip, left-to-right. Stop. (Read Fig. A.13 in this order: a-b-c-d-c-b-a). This is one step of the walk.

To continue the walk, simply repeat the return throws without stopping, eliminating (a) and (e) from Fig. A.13. This should feel much like it did in your hands: left-right-left-right.

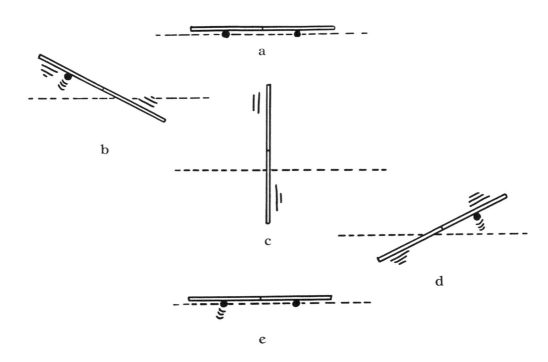

Figure A.13
The Half-Flip. For "Walking," cycle through parts b-c-d-c-b-.

Note: Some instructors prefer to walk on the ground first (i.e., with one end of the baton resting on the floor). Although this does teach you control of the handsticks, it teaches you almost nothing about how the baton will move in the air. Still, if you are uncomfortable using the handsticks, you may wish to begin with a little walking on the ground.

Appendix III
Understanding Juggling

My students often ask me about my unusual classification of juggling styles. While many jugglers are used to grouping sets of tricks by the type of *object* involved, I prefer to group tricks by the type of manipulation being done. So, for example, some Devil Stick tricks are gyroscopic, some are toss juggling, some balancing, and a few are contact juggling tricks (all with the hands replaced).

The reason for my preference is this: by separating the trick from the object, one can more easily grasp the general case and develop new variations. For example: although the trick of rolling a bowler hat down one's arm is virtually identical to doing the same with a volleyball, these two tricks are usually taught separately. One is a "hat" trick, one is a "ball" trick. The student is not encouraged to associate the two—and thereby infer that the same move could be done with other objects (for example, a hoop, a cane, or a dumbbell). This is a trivial example, but others are more subtle.

So here I will present a very brief description of the basic nature of four categories of juggling tricks, along with examples of each, and combination tricks.

Balancing and Setting

One of the simplest forms of juggling is "setting." It is so simple that it is almost always combined with other styles in performance. "Balancing" is slightly harder, and is sometimes done by itself. The difference between balancing and setting is "equilibrium."

Figure A.14
Balancing, from a photo of Ron Meyers.

The three cones in Fig. A.15 illustrate the three basic types of equilibrium. The first is unstable, and it will quickly topple over. It has only one point of contact. The second is stable, as it is "comfortable" where it is, with at least three points of contact. Cone (c) is called "marginally" stable: it might roll, and it might not. All of its contact points are along a straight line, and its center of gravity stays at the same height even if it rolls.

Although cone (c) is an ideal case (one not usually found in nature), its rough equivalent does exist in juggling. A set (stable equilibrium) which is close enough to unstable to be difficult is usually called "marginal." Compare, then, the three cones in Fig. A.15 with their real-life equivalents: unstable, stable, and marginal.

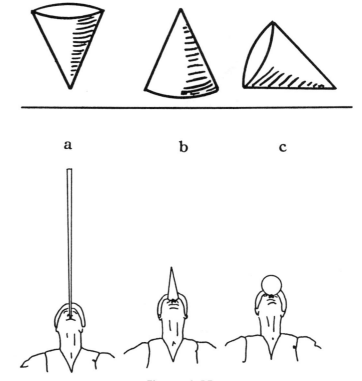

Figure A.15
Three Types of Equilibrium: Unstable, Stable, and Marginal.

•Maintaining the Equilibrium

To maintain a set, you simply need to hold still. If you were *holding* the stick in Fig. A.16, any jerking around would make the ball fall off. More specifically, you must not apply any "breaking" acceleration to the group. Any of the three horizontal pushes in Fig. A.16 might break the set, although (c) is by far the least dangerous. Axial acceleration (Fig. A.16d) is easier for the group to tolerate, which makes stacks of this nature easy to balance, once you let go of them.

To maintain a balance (for example, to keep the stack in Fig. A.16 supported on your chin), you must constantly move the support point to compensate for the object's tendency to fall. This is easiest if you watch the top of the object, since it moves more than any other part when the object sways.

It is easier to set shorter objects, such as salt shakers and golf balls, because they are more stable, having very low centers of gravity. Conversely, it is easier to balance a longer object (one with a higher center of gravity) because longer objects fall out of line more slowly, and are easier

Figure A.16
Breaking a Stack:
Pushes (a) and (b) are much more likely to break the stack than (c), and (d) will have no effect at all.

to follow. Feathers and sheets of paper also fall more slowly, because of their air resistance. Peacock feathers are about the easiest objects to balance, unless you are extremely strong and prefer 30′ ladders.

Gyroscopic Juggling

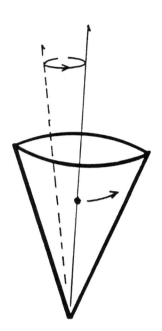

There is another way to maintain cone (a) in Fig. A.15: get it spinning like a top. The spin of the top fights against the inclination (tipping over) like the wheel of a gyroscope. So the effect of a single support point combined with gravitational pull is changed: instead of falling to one side, the top tends to precess (Fig. A.17). By inducing a spin, you have stabilized the cone, or turned a balance into a set.

Although the standard top has a good shape for spinning on the *floor*, it is not the ideal shape for juggling. It has a relatively high center of gravity, which means that it must be spinning very fast to prevent the spin from collapsing. It also slows down quickly because it has a low moment of inertia (the rotational equivalent of mass).

A more ideal shape for spinning is the plate, Fig A.18. Its center of gravity is negligibly higher than the support point, and because of its broad, flat shape it has a better moment of inertia. (To make this moment even larger, more weight should be added to the outer edge.

Figure A.17
Spinning a cone.

Physics instructors demonstrate gyroscopic phenomena using a solid-rubber bicycle tire). Some manufacturers of juggling supplies actually make plates whose center of gravity is *at* or *below* the support point, making the plate stable even when it is not spinning (Fig. A.18b).

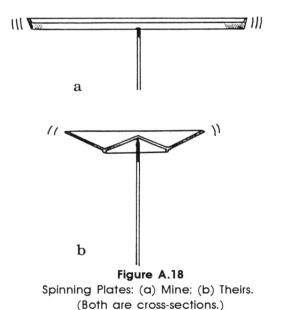

Figure A.18
Spinning Plates: (a) Mine; (b) Theirs.
(Both are cross-sections.)

Spinning balls are more like tops, and at lower speeds they require a bit of balancing to maintain. But a ball spinning at about 150RPM is still a lot more stable than it would be with no spin. Larger balls are much easier to spin (and keep spinning) than small ones, for two reasons. First, they do require a little balancing, and taller objects are easier to balance. Second, they have a much larger moment of inertia.

Some Combination Tricks

A simple combination of balancing and gyroscopics is this: put a spinning plate on a long pole. Balance the pole on your forehead. Since the plate needs absolutely no "attention" once it is on the pole (you could set the pole in an umbrella stand and go out for a sandwich if you wanted to), this is a fairly simple trick. Simpler even than balancing the pole alone, since the plate effectively raises the center of gravity of the entire stack.

A harder trick is to put the end of that pole on the center of another spinning plate (Fig. A.19). Here you have two sets, two spins, and one balance.

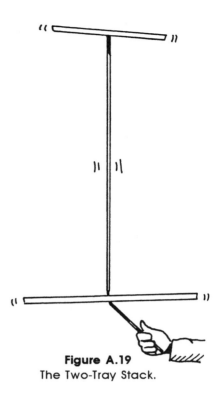

Figure A.19
The Two-Tray Stack.

Toss Juggling

Most "release" moves in baton twirling, plate spinning, hat manipulation, contact juggling, and even football, are versions of toss juggling. Release moves in their purest form compose the bulk of juggling routines with balls, rings, clubs, knives, and scarves. Devil Sticks and cigar box juggling are based on toss juggling with the hands replaced.

The most basic move of toss juggling is the throwing of an object (like a ball) into the air, and catching it. This trick is so simple that several other objects can be thrown and/or caught while the first one is on its way up and back. Theoretically, if things fell slower, it would get even easier.

The Three-Ball Cascade overlaps three simple tosses at regular intervals, like three strands in a braid. For each ball that falls out of the air, another one rises to replace it. Other toss juggling tricks involve three, four, or even more

Figure A.20
Toss Juggling.

objects in the air at once, and even (at times) two or three objects in the same hand. The basic rule seems to be that at least one object should be in the air at all times, but even this rule is sometimes broken (as in the case of one-ball toss juggling).

When toss juggling with non-spheres, the orientation of the objects is also important. A club must fall so that its handle (or whatever part you intend to catch) is in the hand. Two knives should spin so as not to hit each other in mid-air.

Combinations of Toss Juggling and Balancing

Toss a cane, balanced on your hand, into the air, and catch it again in a balance. Throw it for a half-spin and catch it, balanced on the other end.

... and Gyroscopics

Spin a plate on one finger, toss it, and catch it on the same finger of the other hand. Since these are fairly simple throws, you might easily do three plates in a Cascade.

Replacing the Hands

This is probably the most diverse form of juggling, and the one least recognized as a separate style. Although the hands are the most versatile natural tools you have, simpler tricks can be done with simpler things: either various other parts of your body, or tools which you hold in your hands.

The first group of hand replacements is the body. Since balancing a pole is a fairly simple task, it is often performed on the forehead, the chin, the foot, the shoulder, and other places. Balls and other objects (especially hats) can be caught and held

Figure A.21
Fire Devil Sticks, from a photo of the author.

on other parts of the body. Balls are often juggled using the feet, the head, or even the mouth. Batons and canes can be rolled over the legs, shoulders, and back.

The second group involves tools. Spinning a plate on a stick is actually a form of hand replacement, using the stick to replace your finger. In some cases, like this one, the replacement is actually more suited to the task than the hand would be: The stick has a sharp point to better stay in the center of the plate. Other such tricks include: catching a football in a fishnet (toss juggling with hands replaced by net), a vertical propeller with Devil Sticks (toss/gyroscopics with hand replaced by thin dowel), and the yo-yo (gyroscopics with the hand replaced by a long string). In other cases, the hands are replaced by things less useful, thereby making the trick obviously harder. Such cases include the tic-toc walking of Devil Sticks, most cigar box moves, and the ball-on-plate Butterfly variations (Chapter Eight).

The breakdown of juggling tricks into their most basic elements helps us in the invention of new and different tricks, much like finding the prime factors of a large number tells us a lot about that number. Following are a series of tricks (many from this book) and their "prime factors."

1) Balancing a cane on the foot: Balancing, Hand replacement = BH

2) Throwing the cane in (1) from the foot to a balance on the hand: Balancing (on foot), Hand replacement (on foot), Toss juggling, Balancing (on hand). = B^2HT

3) Same as (2) above, except catching in a balance on the chin: Add a second Hand replacement. = B^2H^2T

4) Head Rolls (Chapter Three): Contact Juggling, Hand replaced by head. = CH

5) Standing on one foot: Acrobatics (another group of tricks which are often associated with juggling). = A

6) Toss-and-Grab (Chapter Seven): Contact juggling and Toss juggling. = CT

7) Toss-and-Grab while Standing on one foot: = CTA

8) Toss-and-Grab while on one foot, holding a spinning plate on a stick: = CTA plus Gyroscopics (the plate), and Hand replacement (the stick) = CTAGH

9) Same as (8) above, plus head rolling a third ball: = C^2H^2TAG

10) The Francis Brunn Circus Finish: Standing on the left foot, spinning two hoops on the right leg, spinning two more hoops on the right arm, holding a spinning ball on the right forefinger, juggling three rings in the left hand, and maintaining two balls set on a mouthstick and a forehead pedestal: = $AG^5TH^2S^3$ (unless you count the spinning rings as hand replacements, in which case add another H^4!)

This "prime factors" analysis may seem a bit strange, but it is a good way to quantitatively analyze various juggling tricks.

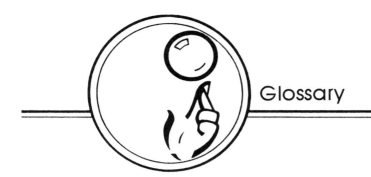 Glossary

Balancing: A type of juggling trick involving the maintenance of an object in unstable equilibrium.

Body Moves: In contact juggling, any trick involving rolling or catching the ball(s) anywhere besides the hands. In other styles, this also includes tricks where the principals or the hands move around other parts of the body. Example: behind-the-back with Devil Sticks (Fig. A.21).

Butterfly: The basic move in one-ball contact juggling, rolling the ball over the fingertips of one hand.

Camelbacking: A vaudevillian term for contact juggling, either with coins or small crystal balls.

Catching Hand: In contact juggling transfers, the hand which receives the ball (see Throwing Hand).

Combination: A compound trick formed by performing two different simpler tricks simultaneously or in quick succession.

Contact Juggling: The graceful manipulation of single objects and object groups.

Control Position: A place on the hand, body, or head where a ball can be caught and held still. The palm is a control position.

Cradle: The control position on the back of the hand, where a ball can be held on the knuckles of two or three fingers.

Devil Sticks: An Oriental form of gyroscopic juggling in which one or more batons are juggled using short sticks to replace the hands.

Diabolo: An Oriental yo-yo. It is not tied to the string, and the string itself is held at both ends, usually tied to a pair of handsticks.

Gyroscopic juggling: A form of juggling which takes advantage of the unusual properties of spinning objects. Examples include plate spinning and the yo-yo.

Lead Hand: In Butterfly transfers, if the hands cross in front of the body, the hand furthest from the body is called the "lead" hand.

Pitch, Throw, and Toss: In this book, "pitch" is reserved to describe a throw that goes straight up. "Throw" and "toss" are interchangeable, although "throwing hand" has a special definition.

Principals: In a juggling trick, the objects being juggled.

Series: A compound trick formed by performing a single simpler trick several times in quick succession.

Set: A type of juggling trick involving the maintenance of an object in stable equilibrium.

Smooth: A place on the hand, head, or body where a ball cannot be reliably caught, stopped, or held.

Stall: A pause in a juggling trick during which at least one hand is inactive.

Throwing Hand: In contact juggling transfers, the hand from which the ball originates, even if it does not fly through the air.

Toss Juggling: A form of juggling in which the principals are thrown into the air and caught, usually in complex patterns.

Tray Plane: (1) In contact juggling, the level plane in which a flat palm spin travels. (2) In toss juggling, the level plane in which the forearms roughly stay during the cascade.

Trick: In juggling, any single manipulation or any series or combination of simpler tricks, performed ostensibly for the entertainment of an audience or for personal amusement.

Wall Plane: An imaginary vertical plane in front of the body within which certain juggling tricks are supposed to stay.

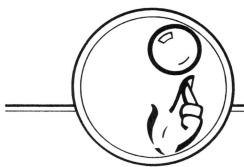

Suggested Reading

Circus Techniques, by Hovey Burgess, with photos by Judy Burgess. New York: Drama Book Specialists, 1976. Provides an excellent overview of basic techniques including: juggling, tumbling, balancing and equilibristics, highwire, and trapeze work.

The Complete Juggler, by Dave Finnegan, illustrated by Bruce Edwards. New York: Vintage Books, 1987. Deals with the basics of just about every style of juggling, plus a discussion of teaching methods and professional juggling.

Passing the Hat, by Patricia Campbell, with photos by Alice Belkin. New York: Delacorte Press, 1981. Available from Brian Dube Juggling Supplies, 25 Park Place, New York, NY 10017. Describes some of the people, places, and tricks of the trade in American street performing.

The Juggling Book, by Carlo. New York: Vintage Books, 1974. One of the first of its kind, it was published in the heyday of tie-die and bellbottoms and contains a lot of good how-to. Great if you like phrases like "watch the balls do their cosmic dance."

Juggling for the Complete Klutz, by John Cassidy and B.C. Rimbeaux, illustrated by Diane Waller. Palo Alto, CA: Klutz Press, 1988. An easy-to-find how-to that comes with its own balls, *Klutz* covers the basics of ball juggling with cute cartoons and small words.

Now You See It, Now You Don't, by Bill Tarr, illustrated by Barry Ross. New York: Vintage Books, 1976. A refreshing and profusely illustrated beginner's guide to sleight of hand magic. Tarr explains a few card, coin, and ball flourishes including fanning, finger rolls, and the (two-ball) Elevator. He also provides a thorough course in basic magic.

Juggling With Finesse, by Kit Summers, illustrated by Tuko Fujisaki. San Diego, CA: Finesse Press, 1987. Possibly the most comprehensive volume for the advanced juggler, *Finesse* includes hundreds of unique tricks and styles, and contains inspiring photos of history's greatest jugglers.

ABOUT THE AUTHOR

James Ernest is a professional juggler and freelance illustrator living in Seattle, Washington. His many hobbies include music, game design, science fiction, and breadmaking. He began teaching and performing juggling at the age of 13.